LEGAL DUTY AND UPPER LIMITS

LEGAL DUTY AND UPPER LIMITS
HOW TO SAVE OUR DEMOCRACY AND PLANET FROM THE RICH

BERND REITER

ANTHEM PRESS

Anthem Press
An imprint of Wimbledon Publishing Company
www.anthempress.com

This edition first published in UK and USA 2021
by ANTHEM PRESS
75–76 Blackfriars Road, London SE1 8HA, UK
or PO Box 9779, London SW19 7ZG, UK
and
244 Madison Ave #116, New York, NY 10016, USA

Copyright © Bernd Reiter 2021

The author asserts the moral right to be identified as the author of this work.

All rights reserved. Without limiting the rights under copyright reserved above, no part of this publication may be reproduced, stored or introduced into a retrieval system, or transmitted, in any form or by any means (electronic, mechanical, photocopying, recording or otherwise), without the prior written permission of both the copyright owner and the above publisher of this book.

British Library Cataloguing-in-Publication Data
A catalogue record for this book is available from the British Library.

ISBN-13: 978-1-78527-637-8 (Hbk)
ISBN-10: 1-78527-637-9 (Hbk)
ISBN-13: 978-1-78527-640-8 (Pbk)
ISBN-10: 1-78527-640-9 (Pbk)

This title is also available as an e-book.

CONTENTS

Preface   vii

Chapter 1	Out of Crisis	1
Chapter 2	Direct Local Democracy and Legal Duty	21
Chapter 3	Predistribution and Upper Limits	45
Chapter 4	Reparations	73
Chapter 5	Conclusions and Implications	93
Final Considerations		109

Notes   113
References and Further Readings   115
Index   133

PREFACE

In this short book, I propose new ways of thinking about, and solving, our current political, economic, and ecological problems. I will show that adopting upper limits to wealth and income, replacing elections with local direct democracy and legal duty, and replacing welfare and redistribution policies with predistribution and reparations promises new solutions to political apathy, discontent, manipulation, economic inequality, and looming ecological disaster.

I perceive the policy suggestions I formulate here as inevitable if we seek to protect and restore justice, fairness, equal opportunity, and liberty, while also securing ecological soundness and keeping free, if limited, markets and market competition. In fact, I cannot perceive of other ways to achieve these goals together. While currently utopian, the proposals I advance and elaborate here offer hope and possibilities and they explicitly stand up against the widespread mantra that "there are no alternatives." This book will show that our collective choices are not reduced to capitalism versus socialism. In fact, both capitalism and socialism have been unable to achieve collective goals while maintaining liberty and ecological soundness. Both are undesirable.

This book will quickly move from an analysis of the current crises of political alienation and manipulation, of unacceptable economic inequality and unfairness, and of the looming ecological disaster, in Chapter 1, toward possible solutions to these problems, presented in Chapters 2, 3, and 4. Chapter 5 will elaborate some of the most likely implications if the policies I suggest were implemented. The Conclusion, finally, offers some reflection on the limitations of this books and possible ways forward.

The remainder of this chapter is dedicated to introducing the crises our world faces today and elaborating the idea of paradigms in our thinking and research. I will conclude this chapter with a call to challenge current paradigms and replace them with new ones, as our old ways of looking at, perceiving, and analyzing the world has proven unable to develop solutions and proposals that stand up to the tremendous tasks ahead of us.

CRISIS

Crisis, according to Thomas Kuhn (1996), leads to scientific revolutions at a point when normal science is no longer able to produce the kind of knowledge that addresses the problems at hand. This is the moment we find ourselves in. Normal (social) science, operating under the paradigms of representative democracy, capitalism, or socialism is unable to capture the problems we face and, as a result, is incapable of producing possible solutions. If science does not offer any solutions to our multiple problems, then our everyday discussions and debates about politics and markets tend to follow suit, as science is supposed to operate as a vanguard for everyday knowledge. We need a shift in paradigms.

Why? You might ask. Here is why: Our democracies are losing their appeal to many voters. The American Congress has had an approval rate of under 30 percent over the past 10 years. In fact, some 75 percent of Americans disapprove of the way political representatives are doing their job. This disapproval has remained constant under changing parties dominating Washington, DC. In many of the established European democracies, mainstream parties are losing more and more supporters. The same is true for many of the less established democracies of Latin America and in parts of Asia. Authoritarian rulers, many of whom we have elected into power, are undermining some of the core values and norms of democratic rule in many countries. Political scandals abound—and yet we don't seem to have good answers to the questions and challenges these problems pose.

Parallel and connected to this democratic crisis is another one, equally severe: our economies have let to tremendous, unacceptable, inequalities in wealth. The 2,000 richest people on our planet own about the same amount of wealth as the rest of us. More precisely, the top 1 percent of people own 50 percent of all assets. The world now counts on some 17 million millionaires—people whose net worth equals or exceeds US $1 million. Why is that a problem and is that really a crisis, you might wonder? It is. Because what rich people can do, which sets them apart from average people, is that they can buy opportunities for themselves and their children. They can send their children to the best private schools and universities. They can provide their offspring with start-up funds, so they can start businesses. They can invest in the stock market and let their money earn their income, multiplying their wealth without any additional effort. Wealth bears more wealth. We are facing a future of a new, global, aristocracy, one that does not have to play by the same rules we all have to abide by because they can buy their way out.

Worse. Once a group of people has been able to create advantages for themselves, there is no catching up to them. If we do nothing, then we will allow the deep division already separating the rich from the rest of us to consolidate. They will win in almost all competitive markets we have to enter during our lifetimes, because they enter them endowed with assets. Their financial capital can buy them other capitals—social, cultural, educational, and residential. Average people already find it very difficult to secure a place in an Ivy League university, to find decent housing, or to get elected into political office. All of these positions are already reserved for the rich. If we do not act now, the world will become more divided; political careers will be reserved even more for the rich; and all the nice places to live will become even more exclusive. Our current economic toolboxes do not contain the necessary tools to fix distortions and manipulations that wealth can achieve, thus making the whole system extremely unfair. If we do nothing, fairness and equal opportunity will be things of the past.[1]

The third crisis we all face is more obvious to most. It is the ecological crisis. If we do nothing, then our children will live in a much-impoverished world with regard to species diversity. More than half of the world's vertebrates have already died out. It will also be a world of increasingly severe storms, droughts, floods, and disasters. Some parts of the world, particularly coastal areas and regions that do not rise high above current sea levels, will be swallowed by the oceans, while all of us will face difficulties finding enough clean water and food. If we do nothing and simply keep going as we have, then our grandchildren might not have a world to live in at all. We are systematically destroying our planet.

Considered together, it becomes clear that we are facing a crisis of overconsumption and of an economization of almost all aspects of life—a colonization of lifeworlds by economic reasoning and instrumental rationality, to use older terms from critical theory. An ever-expanding global economy, based on the sole principle of competition, is destroying our planet and tilting every competition toward those who enter them endowed with more assets. As we have by now transformed almost all of our lifeworlds into competitive systems, unequal asset endowment is undermining fairness and equal opportunity almost everywhere, not just in strictly economic markets. Our schools, universities, residencies, even the quality and accessibility of our healthcare have all been transformed into tiered competitive systems, so that the rich can have an advantage over "the rest," that is, the vast majority of average-earning people or simply people who have to work to make a living.

This transformation went hand-in-hand with a gradual dismantling of anything public and collective. The history of the past four decades has been a history of a gradual loss of human community and a loss of different public spheres. This transformation toward generalized competition was conducted under the guise of enhancing economic efficiency. It resulted in introducing economic reasoning and incentive structures to all spheres of life, even those least suited for competition. However, most competitions are not free and fair at all but influenced by how much information and agency individuals and firms have and how many assets—financial, social, cultural, educational, gendered, and even racial—they bring to the table. When scrutinized, it becomes clear that the true agenda of transforming our world into multitiered competitive systems was driven by those who knew that they will win almost all competitions because they have more assets than the average competitor. These people know that they need not rely on public services and their privileged economic positioning secures them above-average profit opportunities.

It has also become clear that success today depends on the successes of the past. Those who inherited money or other, highly symbolic but yet very real and tangible assets from their ancestors have much better chances to win competitive games today than those who have to start from scratch. Minorities who were barred from even entering competitions over jobs, educational degrees, and desirable housing in desirable neighborhoods until very recently bear the brunt of this historical (dis)accumulation of assets and privilege. They are asked to compete today against those who have abused their ancestors in order to build up the very riches that set them apart today.

Our old ways of thinking about possible solutions fail to offer any promise for our current situation. We need to think about these problems in a new way.

PARADIGMS

Paradigms are broadly accepted ways of seeing and understanding the world. In the sciences, paradigms ensure that collective research and problem-solving efforts come together and support each other. A broadly accepted paradigm ensures that knowledge production that is unorthodox and different from the accepted canon remains unfunded and unpublished and does not reach a broader audience, thus remaining inconsequential. Paradigms ensure and enforce discipline and thus allow for scientific progress as a result of the systematic efforts of many researchers working on the same problems.

Thomas Kuhn has explained, in great detail, what paradigms are and how they operate. He states:

> Men whose research is based on shared paradigms are committed to the same rules and standards for scientific practice. That commitment and the apparent consensus it produces are prerequisites for normal science, i.e., for the genesis and continuation of a particular research tradition.
> (Kuhn, 1996: 11)

Normal science, today, operates within the paradigms of representative democracy and free market competition, with very few exceptions. According to Kuhn, "Normal science does not aim at novelties of fact or theory and, when successful, finds none" (Kuhn, 1996: 52). For a while, socialism was another paradigm, triggering research and problem solving for socialist societies, but since the end of the Cold War and the dissolution of the USSR, socialism has ceased to be a viable, or desirable, paradigm. Liberal, representative democracy and capitalism have become the only game in town. Because of the strength of this paradigm, work produced on alternatives to political representation and capitalism is rare and marginalized. As a result, we are told over and over again that there are no alternatives to the way we currently run our political and economic lives, or that socialism is the only alternative to capitalism. This book shows that there *are* viable alternatives and ways to organize politics and economics, other than socialism, able to avoid the massive concentration of political and economic power among elites we currently experience and also more sustainable and long-lasting.

TURNING THE GAZE AROUND

Most public debates today focus on the poor, on minorities, and on immigrants when discussing the problems of our democracies. The poor, minorities, and immigrants, however, are not our problem. They had no say in designing the kinds of systems that threaten our planet, our well-being, and our social and communal lives. They consume very little and thus have a minimal ecological footprint.

My own research (Reiter, 2019) on just and sustainable political and economic systems instead suggests that it is the superrich who threaten justice, fairness, equal opportunity, and ecological sustainability.

The superrich undermine fairness and equal opportunities in almost all markets they enter because their wealth provides them with a head start. In what is known as "opportunity hoarding," rich parents can buy access to expensive schools and universities for their children, thus ensuring to pass on their privileges. According to Thomas Piketty (2014), the average family income of a student attending Harvard University is $450,000.

The superrich can provide their offspring with start-up funds to launch businesses, and they can secure their access to exclusive clubs and associations where they can meet possible business partners. They can secure the best lawyers, in case they face legal problems. Wealth, in other words, increases educational, economic, social, and even legal opportunities. Civic and political rights and obligations have become stratified so that some people (the rich) have more rights and less obligations toward the collective, while others (the poor and those forced into poverty and mistreatment by discrimination) are left with almost all obligations and few rights. The current COVID-19 crisis has brought this reality into bright light, as those currently working in service jobs are forced to continue to work for all those who can afford to stay at home and get all their goods produced and delivered for them. With COVID-19, the United States has, by many accounts, entered a real-life Hunger Game scenario, where average workers, while constantly vilified by the right, are forced, by law, to continue producing all those products the rich consume.

Due to their excessive consumption, the superrich have a heavy ecological footprint. A 70-meter yacht consumes about 130 gallons of diesel an hour—idling. According to Lucas Chancel and Thomas Piketty (2015), the top 1 percent of Americans produce 50 times as much CO_2e as the world average and 2,500 times as much as the lowest emitters. The rich and the superrich are a major cause of pollution and environmental degradation through their excessive consumption.

Their excessive consumption also creates artificial scarcity for the rest of us, as most markets are finite. If the richest 1 percent of the planet own over 50 percent of all assets, they force 99 percent of people to compete over 50 percent of the remaining assets. Today, the world has over 2,000 billionaires and over 148,000 individuals with a net worth exceeding US $50 million. Their collective influence on our world has been nothing but detrimental.

Politics has long become an exclusive domain of the rich. The average wealth of an US senator was 3.2 million in 2015; that of a member of the house $900,000. Even if not holding office themselves, the superrich are able to influence politicians to pass legislation in their favor, to such an extent that the preferences of average voters have become inconsequential, as Martin Gilens and Benjamin Page (2014) demonstrated in their seminal article.

American democracy is becoming a plutocracy—a system run by the rich. However, the concern about an emerging American aristocracy is as old as the country itself. When the Pennsylvania Declaration of Rights was discussed by the Philadelphia Congress in July and August 1776, it originally contained an article (No. 16), which stated:

> That an enormous Proportion of Property vested in a few individuals is dangerous to the Rights, and destructive of the Common Happiness, of Mankind; and therefore every free State hath the Right by its Laws to discourage the Possession of such Property. (http://founders.archives.gov/documents/Franklin/01-22-02-0314.)

In today's world, it is stock ownership, no longer land ownership, that makes a person rich. So instead of discouraging the concentration of landownership, it is the concentration of securities that should concern us today.

What can be done? French economist Thomas Piketty (2014) has explained that *in theory* markets provide opportunities to catch up with the rich as long as economic growth outpaces returns on capital gains. In the United States, however, real economic growth over the past 10 years has hovered around 3 percent, while stock market returns on the S&P 500 have consistently yielded over 10 percent during the same time period. This means that those of us who had money to invest in the stock market earned on average three to four times as much money as those who worked.[2]

I wrote "in theory," because Piketty does not account for other, real, factors complicating the lives of working people, such as racial and gender bias, class background, and educational levels. If we consider all of those, we realize that work has lost its force to equalize people. In other words, the perverse inequalities of our days will not disappear by themselves over time.

Progressive taxes have been tried, successfully, in this country. It seems difficult to remember that until the 1970s, top earners paid over 70 percent income tax. Taxes on capital gains were capped at 28 percent in 1990 and are now down to 20 percent, but taxing capital gains would certainly contribute to achieving more equal opportunities, as even Warren Buffet suggested.

Taxing the rich would undoubtedly lead to a reduction of the wealth controlled by the top 1 percent. It would not, however, change the scenario of unfair competitions through opportunity hoarding. To address that, inheritance would have to be addressed in an attempt to limit, or avoid, that riches accumulated during a lifetime benefit the children of the deceased. If we value justice, fairness, and equal opportunity, we need to start thinking about new approaches to protect our democracies, our economies, and the environment. We need new paradigms that allow us to analyze our political, economic, and ecological crises from a different angle. This book proposes to consider upper limits to income and wealth, direct democracy and legal duty instead of elections, and predistribution and reparations instead of redistribution and welfare. These three proposals constitute a new paradigm and a fresh perspective. They promise to protect equal opportunity, fairness, and liberty while also guarding the ecosystem against excessive consumption and pollution. They promise to rein in the manipulation caused by professional politicians, and they contain an element of broad political education through active participation. The core idea this book seeks to advance is that we do not really need to rely on political and economic elites and that we would be better off without them.

LIFE BY INSTITUTIONAL DESIGN

We live our lives according to institutional design, that is, nothing in the way we manage and control our collective lives is fixed or given. It is all invented and created, at a specific point in time, when external problems demanded fixing and regulating. However, institutions, once created, have a tendency to persist over time, even if circumstances change. They show a tendency toward inertia. Furthermore, those in power and those benefitting from the way things currently are resist institutional change—even if it costs them, and all of us, a future.

The ways we currently run our political and economic lives are in crisis. The institutions we have created to steer these two systems no longer offer a way to ensure that the will of the people actually becomes policy and that economic freedom translates into equal opportunities and fairness for all. Maybe worst of all, we are at risk of species extinction—animal, plant, and human—if we continue to operate under our current political and economic institutions. Like many institutions created to confront a problem, our dominant democratic and economic institutions have been outgrown by reality and they need adjustment.

To change our dominant political and economic institutions, two conditions need to be met. First, institutional change requires the perception of crisis. Nothing changes if all is well. Note that it is not crisis per se, but the *perception* of crisis, which is a condition for institutional change. If a crisis goes unnoticed, it will not trigger any action. This is why we witness so many conservative politicians denying and downplaying the ecological crisis. They know that once this crisis is undeniable, actions against it will be difficult to block. However, the ecological crisis is real and more and more people on the planet understand that because they already experience it and they demand change. Institutional change to protect the environment and our collective survival must start today. We are collectively moving closer to finally reaching a point where the ecological crisis can no longer be denied. We are very close to reaching the first condition for change.

The second condition for institutional change is not external but inherent in our minds. We need to have clear proposals of different institutions that can regulate and control our collective lives more efficiently, protect us from imminent ecological disaster, protect fairness and equal opportunity, and avoid the extreme inequalities we now face. We need viable alternatives. Political scientists and economists are the experts in this field, together with the other disciplines constituting the social sciences. We look at them for guidance and evidence-backed proposals about how to achieve more justice, democracy, and sustainment.

Currently, however, we are receiving almost no guidance from any of the social sciences. Most social scientists adhere to established research paradigms that are connected to and work in tandem with the political and economic institutions that brought us these problems in the first place. Scientific research occurs in disciplines. The whole purpose of these disciplines is to discipline, that is, to ensure that work is done following established rules, methods, and theories. Anything not meeting the disciplinary standards of currently dominating social scientists will not receive attention. It will not be published and not be funded. This is the situation we currently find ourselves in, with very few exceptions.

Some exceptional scholars have started to think about *Designs for the Pluriverse* (the title of cultural anthropologist Arturo Escobar's (2018) latest book), but even they find it difficult to produce reliable knowledge under the existing paradigm. As a result, a lot of innovation today does not originate from scholars and university professors. It comes instead from "the street." Indigenous people of the Americas have long started to seek political autonomy so they can organize their political and economic lives differently from the colonial systems that surround them. Some neighborhoods have formed local transition movements, creating new currencies to escape the power of corporate banking and many are seeking ways to produce their own food. Many people march and protest, chanting "Yes, we can"—advocating for more direct political influence and self-rule and at times inventing new organizational forms within their own movements as they go along. But even they find it difficult to propose something new. More and more people recognize that change must happen and that something must be done rather quickly—but we find ourselves at a loss with regard to possible solutions and new institutions. After the demise of real socialism, we seem to have reached the end of political ideologies, thus leaving representative democracy and capitalism as the default options.

Even the best and latest analysis of political crisis, offered by such prominent political scientists as Larry Diamond (2019) and Yascha Mounk (2019) fall very short of capturing the true magnitude of our current problems—and they contain no promising remedies. Anything produced under the old political and economic paradigm must necessarily fall short of true innovation. Not surprisingly, all Diamond has to offer is to call upon the United States to embrace its democratic traditions and defend democracy worldwide, whereas Mounk proposes the same recipes that other social democrats before him have proposed for centuries: taxes, redistribution, and increased welfare spending. The fact that the books by these authors received such high praise from among their professional colleagues while the social democratic party is losing its status as a majority party in many countries in Europe indicates how far academia has fallen behind reality. The top professors, working in the most elite universities of the world (Stanford and Johns Hopkins, in this case), able to publish their work in the most prestigious publishing houses of the world (here: Penguin and Harvard University Press) are not able to produce anything new—despite all the pressure to do so.

In fairness, however, I must highlight that very recently some extraordinary scholars started producing new work on democratic and economic governance that has also greatly inspired this book. Jacob Hacker (2011) has coined the term "predistribution" and I take inspiration from his work. James Fishkin (2018) has developed a system of deliberative polling, which allows for a detailed assessment of the potential and conditions for successful citizen deliberation and sortition. Michael Neblo, Kevin Esterling, and David Lazer (2018) have also proposed innovative ways to bring elected officials and average citizens together and thus to bridge the gap normally separating rulers from ruled. Michael Neblo (2015) has elaborated the potential of citizen deliberation previously, pointing out many new and exciting possibilities of direct citizen involvement in politics. Beth Noveck (2015) has coined the term "crowdsourcing" and shows how technology can be used to involve average citizens in democratic governance. Tim Jackson (2009) has offered institutional recipes to achieve *Prosperity without Growth*, the title of his book, mostly focused on reduced economic activity and working hours.

Many of these books refer back to a previous generation of scholars who have produced highly influential proposals about how to replace elected officials with randomly selected citizens. Ernest Callenbach and Michael Phillips (2008) originally published their book on a *Citizen Legislature* in 1985, in which they proposed to replace the American House of Representatives with a Representative House of randomly selected citizens. Keith Sutherland proposed replacing the British House of Commons with a House of randomly selected citizens while reining in the power of appointed ministers. In this, by his own account, Sutherland follows the work of James Harrington, who published *Oceana* in 1656. Kevin O'Leary, finally, published his *Saving Democracy* in 2006 and proposes very similar measures to those I am proposing here, namely to replace the lower house of a bicameral political system with an entity of randomly selected citizens. The work of all these pioneers is strongly influencing my own thinking, and writing on this issue.

On the economic front, I build on the work of Jacob Hacker, whom I have already quoted above, as well as on the book of the late Tony Atkinson entitled *Inequality* (2015). The work of Martin O'Neill and Thad Williamson (2014) on *Property-Owning Democracy*, as well as the book by Eric Nelson (2004) on *The Greek Tradition in Republican Thought* certainly inspired my own thinking on this matter. So did the work of John Rawls, Brian Barry, James Tully, and Amartya Sen.

Most of the inspiration for this book comes, however, from "the street"— that is, from people protesting and marching against the political and economic status quo almost everywhere. I also found very inspiring examples of political and economic innovation among Native Americans in North and South America, as well as among the indigenous people of Africa. I owe thanks to them all and I am indebted to their pioneering praxis. As I want this book to be as accessible as possible, I have refrained from the usage of long citations, quotations, and footnotes in hopes to present a more readable book. Should the reader be interested in exploring some of these issues further and in more debt, I have created a bibliography of literature elaborating political and economic institutional innovation and would like to refer the interested reader to it.

CHANGE IS IN THE AIR

Crisis, as I mentioned above, triggers such paradigm shifts and we can already see the first signs. More and more people are discontent with the way their democracies and markets work—or do not work for them. The youth has taken to the streets of the world demanding more decisive action to avert dramatic climate change. They protest. In the middle of this protest, some visionaries propose new solutions and different ways of addressing these problems. This is the time we find ourselves in. I cannot claim that the paradigm shift and possible solutions I suggest in this book are all born in my mind alone. They are "in the air," or maybe "in the streets."

Most of my proposals grow out of my research as a social scientist working on indigenous governance in Latin America. It is there, among native, or first people, that the most promising political, economic, and ecological solutions are practiced (Reiter, 2019). By dwelling on solutions from the Global South, this book also seeks to make a contribution to the very important task of decolonizing our knowledge and our knowledge production. It is, after all, the Global North, or the colonizing "West," that has created our current political and economic systems—and then forced them onto the rest of the world through colonization. The time for Western triumphalism and the belief that the West has, or is, the cure for the rest of the world has run its course as it becomes more and more obvious that the opposite is indeed the case.

It is my hope that this book can help disseminate this new paradigm so that other researchers can elaborate its consequences and implications in more detail. Before we get there, enough people have to embrace it and kick the old paradigm out, as different paradigms cannot coexist. For the new to live, the old must die.

CHAPTER 1

OUT OF CRISIS

In this chapter, I elaborate the background for the proposals I will advance in the chapters to follow. Crisis, it is often said, can lead to opportunities, and I firmly believe that the current crises of democracy, politics, economics, and the ecology are severe enough to propel many into a mode of intensive solution seeking. However, I also fear that our current modes of looking and thinking about possible solutions to these crises are not adequate for actually finding any. We need to change our way of looking, thinking, and analyzing our current problems and adopt a new angle, or prism, allowing us to see things afresh. We need a shift of paradigms, as I will argue here. Once we apply these new paradigms, I am hopeful that new solutions will become apparent.

DEMOCRATIC CRISIS

Our democracies are in crisis. Not just in the United States but almost everywhere on the planet. Disenchantment with politics and politicians is on the rise, fanning the voices of extremists. Right-wing pundits, some of whom elected officials, are able to seduce more and more people with their rhetoric of blaming others, mostly immigrants and minorities, for the problems caused by political and economic elites. Leaders like Donald Trump, Viktor Orban, and Jair Bolsonaro succeed by dividing people and communities, pitching them against each other. Without a united, vibrant, observant, vigilant, and actively involved public, political elites are able to rule with less and less restraint. Democracy, the "rule of average people," is distorted into a farce and average people, who supposedly are the sovereign in a democracy, are made to believe that democracy consists of irrational bickering. The more such rulers succeed in dividing the citizenry, the more democracy loses its foundation and the easier it becomes for those in power to rule without consent, to manipulate without restraint, and to lie without remorse. The true agenda of rulers like Trump, Orban, and Bolsonaro is to undermine democracy by dividing and undermining the public sphere. A public sphere in shambles, with people at each other's throats over differences of opinion, opens the door for despotism.

With Trump, Orban, and Bolsonaro, we have entered a historical phase of anti-public politics or non-politics, where private profits not only dominate the political agenda, but where they also control the public agenda and systematically undermine dialogue, tolerance, and mutual respect—the pillars of democratic governance. Instead of a politics for all, we are witnessing a politics for friends, family, and allies—and against all those who disagree. In Trump's America, it is also clear who his friends and allies are; his own family and fellow billionaires, some of whom he has appointed to political office, while enacting the largest corporate tax cuts in recent history for the others. What unites all three, and similar others of our time, is their disdain for the press, often coined "lying press" in a sad, but revealing, similative to the Nazi coinage of this term ("Lügenpresse"), their systematic ignoring of science and technical expertise, and their active dismantling and hollowing out of institutions serving the public interest.

Trump, Bolsonaro, and Orban are symptoms of our democratic crisis and a faltering democratic fabric that can bring people with diverse opinions together to find compromise. They are also the ones driving divisions even further and undermining public and collective agendas. Among the most revealing aspects of their rule is their active attempt to disenfranchise the citizens for whom they are supposed to act. Trump, in May 2020, threatened to withhold federal funding from Michigan and Nevada when these two states sought to enact voting by mail in times of COVID-19. Earlier in 2020, the Wisconsin legislator insisted on holding in-person elections in April 2020, in the middle of COVID-19 and against the recommendation of its democratic governor who had proposed voting by mail. Trump and other Republican rulers were recorded expressing their goal to disenfranchise segments of society in order to secure their rule.

In the absence of broad citizen participation, oversight, and control, many of those controlling our destinies are not elected at all. Ivanka Trump and Jared Kushner advise the American president, but have no qualifications, or mandates, to do so. Presidential appointees to high public office, such as Betsy DeVos or former presidential advisor John Bolton, were invested with making decision for the American people without mandate and, in many cases, any apparent qualifications. President Donald Trump himself did not win the popular vote in his elections—an election that only counted on the participation of 58.1 percent of eligible American voters, 46.1 percent of which voted for him. Of a total of 280 million eligible American voters, Donald Trump received 62,984,828 votes—less than 23 percent.

Despite this very thinly spread democratic legitimacy of the president, his family members like Jared Kushner have the influence to fan war, which can cost thousands of lives and bring about unspeakable suffering. People like Jared Kushner, of course, will not join the war themselves or send his own children to fight and he and his family will not suffer personal harm. The same is true for many elected officials. While most lack the kind of power of a Jared Kushner, they still make very consequential decisions for others, affecting and implicating their lives. Those others, the average people of a country, have entrusted elected officials and state bureaucrats with an awesome power, trusting and hoping that they "do the right thing" and act in the public's best interest. The only power average people have in such a system is to not elect those again who did not act in the electorate's best interest—every two, four, or six years—and hope for the best in the meantime.

AGAINST REPRESENTATION

Given population growth, each representative in the American House of Representatives now represents some 800,000 citizens on average. It is very difficult to imagine, even theoretically, how exactly such a representation could possibly work and what it means.

Some analysts of political representation have indeed argued that political representation and democracy are not related at all and that representation and voting work *against* democracy. David van Reybrouck (2018), for example, has entitled his book on democratic innovations *Against Elections*. Prominent American political theorist Hanna Pitkin explained in 2004 that "representation, at least as a political idea and practice, emerged only in the early modern period and had nothing at all to do with democracy" (Pitkin, 2004: 337). She concludes, "The arrangements we call 'representative democracy' have become a substitute for popular self-government, not its enactment" (Pitkin, 2004: 340).

Harvard law professor Lawrence Lessig (2019) has shown that political representatives today only represent the rich. Marina Sitrin and Dario Azzellini (2014) have argued the same even before that in *They Can't Represent Us*—the title of their book. They argue that there is a global movement against representative democracy already on its way, finding expression in such movements as *Podemos!*, The Zapatistas, and the *Ya Basta!* Protests.

Hannah Arendt, probably the most famous post–World War II political theorist, had already argued in 1965 that "representative government has in fact become oligarchic government. [...] The age-old distinction between ruler and ruled which the Revolution had set out to abolish through the establishment of a republic has asserted itself again; once more, the people are not admitted to the public realm, once more the business of government has become the privilege of the few" (Arendt, 1965: 273, 240). Hanna Pitkin, probably the most known contemporary analysts of political representation has argued in 2004 that "Despite repeated efforts to democratize the representative system, the predominant result has been that representation has supplanted democracy instead of serving it. Our governors have become a self-perpetuating elite that rules—or rather, administers—passive or privatized masses of people. The representatives act not as agents of the people but simply instead of them" (Pitkin, 2004: 339).

Michael Saward, another prominent political scientist, has added his voice to this critical canon. His diagnosis is similar to the ones voiced by Arendt and Pitkin:

> There can be little doubt that the time is ripe for revisiting the idea of representation. In a number of countries, not least many established Western democracies, and in regional and international bodies, there is a great deal of real concern about its practice. Voters are disaffected and voting rates are in decline. Political leaders and parties face high levels of cynicism and distrust. Many groups do not feel that their views are properly represented, or at least not in mainstream politics. In this context, can representation still be democratic? (Saward, 2008: 1000)

Saward dwells on another specialist on this issue, Andrew Rehfeld (2006), who has plausibly demonstrated that democracy and representation are not related. Saward also agrees with Pitkin that the idea and practice of representation are not old. He writes, "It was only with what Dahl (1989) calls the 'second transformation' of democracy that our modern understanding of 'representative democracy'—as a system in which the people choose the rulers at regular intervals in elections, combining elements of democratic choice with political representation—began to take shape" (Saward, 2008: 1001).

The classic verdict against political representation comes from French philosopher Jean-Jacques Rousseau (1712–78). For Rousseau, "the moment a people allows itself to be represented, it is no longer free: it no longer exists" (Rousseau, 2003 [1762]: 66). Rousseau explains:

the idea of representation is modern; it comes to us from feudal government, from that iniquitous and absurd system which degrades humanity and dishonors the name of man. In ancient republics and even in monarchies, the people never had representatives; the word itself was unknown. It is very singular that in Rome, where the tribunes were so sacrosanct, it was never imagined that they could usurp the functions of the people, and that in the midst of so great a multitude they never attempted to pass on their own authority a single plebiscitum. (Rousseau, 2003 [1762] : 65)

For Rousseau, lawmaking is the crucial element of democracy and it is lawmaking, in particular, that cannot be delegated. He writes, "Law being purely the declaration of the general will, it is clear that, in the exercise of the legislative power, the people cannot be represented" (Rousseau, 2003 [1762]: 65). Thus, according to Rousseau, what makes a republic democratic is not the fact that citizens elect representatives, but rather that citizens themselves make the laws they live under.

The problem we face, then, is that we need to rethink political representation, but we do not have any models or ideals that can guide such a rethinking. Political representation and democracy are, however, not linked and the first step we need to take when rethinking democracy is to decouple it from political representation. Indeed, the idea of political representation only enters the scene through Thomas Hobbes's *Leviathan*, first published in 1651. From there, it inspired the architects of both the French and the American Republics—particularly the latter, whose architects had the explicit intent to limit the power of ordinary people. While one might understand the fear of aristocrats and the "educated upper crust" of the likes of Hobbes, Sieyes, Hamilton, and Madison against "mob rule," we must ask ourselves if those fears justify the dominant system of political representation today.

The essence of political representation was then and continues to be to hand over the power of the masses to the few who are "better equipped" to decide "for all of us." However, recent history rather indicates that instead of deciding in our best interest, our lawmaking representatives make laws that do not necessarily favor all of us. We are also facing the question if we are indeed served well with more and more laws and if lawmaking indeed needs to be done by professionals. Finally, as politics is becoming less rational and more focused on culture, identity, and emotion, the question arises about how to foster and cultivate practical political knowledge among a broader citizenry. And while all of these questions are as old as the discipline of political science itself, it is only now becoming clear that political representation itself is to be blamed for the spreading of political disinterest and the widespread trumping of conspiracy theories over scientific, researched, and rational explanation. It is also the cause for the growing importance of fake news and disinformation over facts. The less we, as a people, participate in political decision-making, the less practical knowledge about politics will we acquire and the more will we be exposed to manipulations of our opinions by the media. Political representation has brought us massive political ignorance and it has exposed us all to the manipulation of powerful media, controlled and directed in the interest of the few. The time has come to rethink the legislative branch of government and its relation to, or mediation with, the people of a country.

AGAINST VOTING

Voting has an important place in all democracies, for a reason. Not all collective decisions we make will be unanimous—and they should not be. Disagreement and dissent are part of democratic societies and dissenters as well as minority opinion-holders must be protected against a potential "tyranny of the majority" (Mouffe, 2013). However, among those who practice politics, and hence democracy, for us today, that is our elected officials, voting is supposed to be preceded by debate and deliberation. Deliberation, as I will explain further down, is a necessary and central ingredient of democratic decision-making. Voting is supposed to be reserved for situations where no agreement can be reached among deliberating peers (Manin, 1997; Mansbridge, 1980).

Instead, contemporary democracies around the globe have elevated voting, particularly the election of political representatives, to the main and oftentimes the only criterion of democracy. It appears that we are happy and satisfied with a country's democracy if leaders are elected in free elections. While universal suffrage is important, democracy's reduction to voting is not. Voting, per se, is not central to democracy—only to representative democracy. Representative democracy however, as I have argued above, is inherently problematic.

What is indeed central to democracy is participation (Barber, 1984; Pateman, 1970). All citizens need to be actively involved in the running of their own public affairs for a system to be truly democratic. Voting is but a small and technical component of selecting public officials and it was never considered, for example by the ancient Greeks, as the most democratic. In Athens and other Greek city-states of European antiquity, selection by lottery was perceived as the most democratic way of selecting public officials.

The promotion and spread of voting and elections as the central components of democracies must be attributed to the spread of US hegemony in the world, as it was under the guidance and leadership of the United States, either after major wars or after successful invasions, when minimalist versions of elite democracy were implemented, or implanted, in the world. This was so in Germany and Japan after World War II and it continues to be the case in Iraq and Afghanistan today.

In the eyes of most American foreign policy experts, it is precisely political representation, and not democracy, that brought stability to such countries as Germany and Japan and thus has the potential to achieve the same in Latin America, the Middle East, and Asia. After all, average German people were found to be deeply undemocratic in their value systems by such prominent political scientists and American government advisors as Gabriel Almond and Sidney Verba (1963), who advised not only the US Department of State but also other US foreign policy agencies. So did their colleague, prominent political scientist Samuel Huntington, who argued in 1968 that political participation by the masses leads to political instability in emerging democracies. Huntington even favored authoritarian government for the sake of stability over democracy in all those places where average people could not be entrusted, according to Huntington, to create systems where private property and capitalism were safe and protected. Almost all US interventions in Latin America and the Caribbean during the twentieth century were driven by the US government's suspicion and fear of the mostly poor and nonwhite masses of those countries coming to political power.

The profoundly racist idea that average people, but particularly the poor and nonwhites, could not be entrusted with running their own governments had a stunning revival when the United States took it on itself to "bring democracy" to such countries as Iraq and Afghanistan, as there average people were not only poor and nonwhite—they were also Muslims. The agenda of US foreign policy with regards to "bringing democracy" to such places as Iraq and Afghanistan is clear: instead of a system controlled by average people, the United States seeks to implement minimal democratic systems so that pro-US elites can conduct pro-US policies even against the will of the majority. A case in point is Afghan president Ashraf Ghani who before taking the Afghan presidency was an American citizen and professor of anthropology at Johns Hopkins University. He also worked for the World Bank. What the United States is seeking to implant abroad is not democracy understood as rule by average people. It is representative democracy, understood as rule by pro-US-elected elites who ensure that their countries stay open for American business. The reduction of democracy to the free election of political rulers must be seen as a tool to secure stability, not democracy understood as self-rule. Stability, in turn, means the stability to conduct business. With voting participation at a minimum and media manipulation and fake news at a high, such systems can only claim to be democratic in a very narrow, and perverted, sense of this term.

With US hegemony, political representation and the voting into office of pro-Western and pro-American elites became the recipe and blueprint for how democracy is supposed to work and look like in the world. It is, however, an approach informed first and foremost by the profound suspicion of the American political class against average people, poor people, nonwhites, and non-Christians. Madison was motivated by the same fears as most contemporary US foreign policy experts so that the Madisonian model of indirect, representative democracy became the model for the world.

However, voting the supposedly "smarter" or "better equipped" among us into political power is not only failing in Iraq and Afghanistan. Even in the United States, it is hardly the smartest among us who win political office. It is, routinely, the taller candidates winning over the shorter one. Candidates with more hair are routinely favored over those who are bald. Gender bias favors men over women; racism works against African Americans, Latinxs, and Asians, and religious bias raises suspicions against non-Christians. Politicians have long given up saying what they think. They instead say what their pollsters tell them to say, seeking to appeal to the opinion of the undecided median voter and thus undermining the viability of reaching informed decisions from controversial debate. The whole idea that power holders in a democracy are supposed to act on behalf of the citizens who elected them has been reversed into a game of money, media manipulation, and showmanship. Representation and rational decision-making in politics is a thing of the past. Instead of popular sovereignty, our current democratic systems have brought us elite sovereignty *from* the people.

Things are not better in Europe. In the 2019 EU elections, some 400 million EU citizens had the right to cast a vote. Of those 61.5 percent actually voted. That was the highest participation in decades. The same trend is visible in almost all established democracies: more and more people abstain from voting, because they either think that their vote does not matter or because they cannot identify a suitable candidate or party whom to support. A growing number of those who do vote support nontraditional parties in parliamentary systems, thus giving rise to such radical parties as the AfD in Germany or Fidesz in Hungary, or nontraditional candidates, such as Donald Trump, in two-party systems like in the United States.

All of this is very distant from the way "democracy" was first institutionalized, in ancient Athens, and even further removed from the way most humans organized themselves for thousands of years, before the Neolithic revolution, some twelve thousand years ago. Among hunters and gatherers to this day, people make collective decisions involving all, instead of delegating political power to a selected, or elected, few. Many indigenous communities around the world also proceed this way. For some two hundred thousand years, that is how we as a species have ruled ourselves—collectively, with the broad participation of all.

Once institutionalized in ancient Athens, democracy meant "rule of average people" and implied that most political offices and most collective decisions were made by large groups of citizens. While among hunters and gatherers people ruled themselves, in ancient Athens, institutions were invented that allowed for a rotation of office holding and it ensured that if people do not rule themselves all the time, at least citizens (thus excluding women, slaves, and foreigners, in the case of ancient Athens) got a chance to rule at some point in their lives.

From a longue-durée viewpoint, human groups have ruled themselves for most of our history. With the Neolithic revolution and settlement into larger towns and cities, some started to rule over others—kings, chiefs, or, at times, groups of them, declaring themselves aristocrats, that is, better people. Rule over others, however, only became consolidated some five thousand years ago, with the emergence of the first states in Mesopotamia—and it never went uncontested (Scott, 2017). States, after all, as James Scott shows (2017, 2009), were created to rule, exploit, and domesticate people and bring them under the control of elites.

Established democracies today, advanced or not, still rely on the same model of elite states controlling the masses for the sake of extracting profits from them in the form of taxes and obligations. The division of rulers and ruled has not changed—even if now, we elect those who rule us. Most established democracies today have systems where we still elect those whom we deem better, or better suited, to conduct politics for us. By this account, most established democracies are really electoral aristocracies, or "audience democracies," in the words of a prominent analysis of contemporary democracies, Bernard Manin (1997).

Today, we continue to adhere to a system that was invented to avoid genuine self-rule and rule by average people—despite the many changes all our societies have gone through over the past millennia. While politics never required special or expert knowledge, it has become entirely illegitimate to claim today that some of us are "better" than others or better suited for public office. The time for Plato's "philosopher kings"—if there ever was one—has clearly come to an end with the spread of literacy and rising educational levels everywhere. We are all able to be philosopher queens and kings today and it is very doubtful that we need to become philosophers to rule ourselves, because politics, again, does not require special or expert knowledge. This is so simply because nobody knows better what is good for you than yourself. Rule for and over others is inherently problematic and ultimately illegitimate.

ECONOMIC CRISES: THE END OF FAIRNESS AND EQUAL OPPORTUNITY

Most markets are in crisis too. Inequalities have reached new heights, unseen for the past 100 years. The richest 1 percent of people now own 50 percent of all assets on the planet. Amid all the riches, poverty still plagues too many people. While some have far too much to ever spend in 100 lifetimes, others still are unable to feed their families. The American billionaire Warren Buffett famously found that "there's class warfare, all right, but it's my class, the rich class, that's making war, and we're winning." The superrich make their money not through work. Instead, they let their money work for them, a euphemism for making profits while not working at all. According to Thomas Piketty, "Past a certain threshold, all large fortunes, whether inherited or entrepreneurial in origin, grow at extremely high rates, regardless of whether the owner of the fortune works or not" (Piketty, 2014: 309).

Extreme concentrations of wealth have created scenarios where the superrich have withdrawn from most common markets while the "rest" of us—the majority—are facing more and more competition, from more and more people. Capitalist, free market "development," instead of bringing us more free time and leisure, has instead produced a never-ending rat race of more and more people competing harder and harder over scarce resources. Without imposing limits and thus limiting competition, there is no end in sight. The US economist Fred Hirsch already explained in 1976 that most private consumption bears a social component so that the amount of satisfaction gained from it is reduced when too many people share in:

> Advance in society is possible only by moving to a higher place among one's fellows, that is, by improving one's performance in relations to other people's performances. If everyone stands on tiptoe, no one sees better. Where social interaction of this kind is present, individual action is no longer a sure means to fulfill individual choice: the preferred outcome may be attainable only

through collective action. (We all agree explicitly or implicitly not to stand on tiptoe). (Hirsch, 1976: 5)

In other words, if we do nothing, free market competition will lead to more and more relational competition. At the same time, free market competition is already leading to heightened concentrations of wealth and political power and it will press all those who are not in power and not millionaires into stiffer and stiffer competition. More effort, time, and preparation are already required by today's generation to achieve the same goals their parents and grandparents achieved much easier and quicker. Future generations will have to compete even harder and invest even more just to obtain the same outcomes we are achieving today. Average jobs today already require a college degree—when two generations ago, a high school diploma was sufficient. What yesterday required a BA, today demands an MA and tomorrow will require an MA from an elite university or a PhD. There is no end of competition in sight. The promise of capitalism, at least for average people, is turning upside down.

Making matters worse is the tendency of the rich to protect their inherited privileges by withdrawing their assets from general market competition, thus diminishing the total amount of goods in circulation, or at least, effectively in circulation, as most of this market withdrawal is achieved through pricing. As the top 1 percent owns 50 percent of assets, tradeable assets for the 99 percent are drastically reduced.

The "upper crust," in other words, has created separate markets for themselves and shields it from the average wage earner through high pricing. Today, 70 million superrich people compete on markets containing $185 trillion, while the "rest" of us, some 7 billion people, complete on markets of the same size. Who, do you think, competes harder? Asset concentration and asset withdrawal from regularly accessible markets thus creates artificial scarcity, poverty, and exclusion.

Asset concentration over generations has distorted most markets to the point that no fair competition is possible. According to Thomas Piketty (2014), the United States has become an inheritance society: "a society characterized by both a very high concentration of wealth and a significant persistence of large fortunes from generation to generation" (Piketty, 2014: 249). Piketty further explains that

> Whenever the rate of return on capital is significantly and durably higher than the growth rate of the economy, it is all but inevitable that inheritance

(of fortunes accumulated in the past) predominates over savings (wealth accumulated on the present). In strict logic, it could be otherwise, but the forces pushing in this direction are extremely powerful. The inequality $r > g$ in one sense implies that the past tends to devour the future: wealth originating in the past automatically grows more rapidly, even without labor, than wealth stemming from work, which can be saved. Almost inevitably, this tends to give lasting, disproportionate importance to inequalities created in the past, and therefore to inheritance. (Piketty, 2014: 267)

The fortunes the rich inherited from the past not only buy them large houses and a place on the beaches of this world, but it can also buy a better education for their children and, with it, cement privilege firmly into a family history. Before they go to Harvard, Princeton, Yale, Stanford, Columbia, Penn, Brown, Dartmouth, Cornell, Oxford, or Cambridge, the rich send their children to private preschools, middle schools, high schools, or boarding schools where their offspring gets groomed for their bright futures. A Harvard law degree costs US $164,550 in tuition alone (assuming three years of attendance at currently $54,850 of estimated tuition costs for nine months). Jared Kushner, President Donald Trump's son-in-law and thus senior advisor to the American president, apparently was able to study at Harvard because his father donated US $2.5 million to this institution. He then was able to take up graduate studies at NYU, because his father donated US $3 million (Packer, 2020). In 2019, 43 percent of white students admitted to Harvard were "athletes, legacy students, children of faculty and staff, or on the dean's interest list—applicants whose parents or relatives have donated to Harvard" (National Bureau of Economic Research, September 2019: https://www.nber.org/papers/w26316.pdf).

Access to education, knowledge, training, and skills is the most widely recognized path toward undoing inequality—if historically underprivileged groups and individuals actually had access to high quality education. What we witness instead in most countries on the planet is just the opposite: privileged education tends to be reserved for the already privileged, while poor education is extended to the poor. Inherited privilege becomes entrenched, together with inherited exclusion.

The current scenario is one where average people, with average incomes and average wealth, only have a fair chance on most competitive markets if they entered them early—before they became crowded—and then held on to their assets for generations, which is highly unlikely; or if the playfield is leveled for them by a severe crisis. In other words, the current capitalist system is so irrational that crisis is the only hope we have to gain access to most disputed goods and assets. As Joseph Schumpeter (1976) already explained in the 1940s, capitalism relies on "creative destruction."

While the majority of people thus face a world of ever-increasing competition over resources made artificially scarce by the overconsumption of the rich, the rich reap personal benefits they have not earned and do not deserve. By some estimates, up to 80 percent of individual wealth rests on historically accumulated knowledge, the infrastructure, the educational system, the system of law, and other collective and social goods all of us inherited from the past and all of us invest in when paying taxes. This fact can be grasped easily by comparing the chances of economic success of the average American or European to a citizen from a country of the Global South, where such accumulated benefits are not available.

Herbert Simon, the American Nobel laureate of economics, called this inherited wealth "patrimony." Prominent American political scientist Robert Dahl (1982) asked, "Who has made a larger contribution to the operation of General Electric—its chief executives or Albert Einstein or Michael Faraday or Isaac Newton?" (quoted in Alperowitz and Daly, 2008: 126). Gar Alperovitz and Lew Daly (2008) indeed show that many economists and political scientists, including such luminaries as the already-mentioned Herbert Simon and Robert Dahl, and also Thorstein Veblen, George Akerlof, Kenneth Arrow, Douglass North, Richard Posner, Frank Knight, and Brian Barry all recognized that individual achievement today, and hence wealth, is based to a large extent on our common inheritance of accumulated knowledge. G. D. H Cole has called this inheritance a "social dividend" and such economists as Robert Solow, Edward Denison, and Joel Mokyr have accounted for its magnitude. The appropriation of this social dividend by the rich is neither justified nor fair, as it is not based on their efforts alone. No S&P 500 CEO "deserves" to earn over three hundred times more than his or her average employee.

THE ECOLOGICAL CRISIS: OVERCONSUMING OUR WAY INTO ECOLOGICAL COLLAPSE

Another, related side effect of growth and never-ending competition is its impact on our shared ecosystem. More and more competition and an exclusive focus on ever-expanding growth is undermining the very subtract of life: our joint ecosystem. We are collectively heading toward a world with less and less species variety, growing disasters, and looming planetary collapse. The scenarios caused by an average global warming of the planet of just 2 degrees—the maximum agreed upon in the Paris accords in 2016—are horrific. A warming of the planet beyond 2 degrees, which is very likely given that none of 55 most polluting countries have been able to stick to the Paris guidelines so far, resembles a Hollywood production of Armageddon with sea levels rising above 6 feet, wildfires burning year around, droughts devastating fertile lands, hurricanes and tornados causing devastation every year, and temperatures in the tropics too high for human survival—all before 2100 (Wallace-Wells, 2019). Our planet suffers from our excessive and unsustainable consumption and yet the only way we are currently able to conceive of our future on this planet is "development," that is, the transformation of every living system into an economic system molded after the United States and Europe. Growth is the only policy our current models produce when thinking about poverty, where poverty itself is elevated to the sole measure of well-being, thus reducing human, animal, and plant life to only one dimension: economic turnaround.

Instead of successfully helping those in need and protecting those lifeworlds that were stable and satisfying to all those involved, what our policies really have achieved over the past 50 years is not only more consumption for the poor, lifting some of them out of poverty, but an overall economic expansion, reaching a global GDP of some US $80 trillion in 2020, up from $38 trillion in 1990 (https://www.worldometers.info/gdp/). We are reaching the maximum carrying capacity of the planet, as even today, humanity is consuming more resources than the planet is able to produce every year. Current consumption patterns would require 1.7 earths every year (https://www.footprintnetwork.org).

North America and Europe together still account for over 50 percent of the global GDP, with only 14.3 percent of the world population. Economic activity is the most salient reason for global warming, but our current paradigms do not let us envision any solutions to the widening gap separating economic growth and ecological survival.

This reality, however, still seems not enough to bring those in power to take decisive action to ensure our collective survival. Most politicians seem to simply ignore the demands by the youth of this planet for ecologically sound policies.

THE RULING CLASS

The ecological crisis evidences probably most clearly that most political elites have become a ruling class, conducting politics not for the sake of the people or the public good, but for their own sake and narrow interest. Gaetano Mosca described the ruling class in his famous book already in 1939:

Among the constant facts and tendencies that are to be found in all political organisms, one is so obvious that it is apparent to the most casual eye. In all societies—from societies that are very meagerly developed and have barely attained the dawnings of civilization, down to the most advanced and powerful societies—two classes of people appear—a class that rules and a class that is ruled. The first class, always the less numerous, performs all political functions, monopolizes power and enjoys the advantages that power brings, whereas the second, the more numerous class, is directed and controlled by the first; in a manner that is now more or less legal, now more or less arbitrary and violent, and supplies the first, in appearance at least, with material means of subsistence and with the instrumentalities that are essential to the vitality of the political organism. (Mosca, 1939: 50)

The division of rulers and ruled has indeed been with us ever since humans started settling in cities and it was always accepted as the way things need to be, given the assumed unpreparedness of the masses to rule themselves (Scott, 2017). This justification for elite rule, however, has run its course and lost all its legitimacy with the spread of universal education. No longer can the rulers legitimize their rule by highlighting their "superior" knowledge or education. Political representation can no longer count on democratic legitimacy—if they ever had any, as even classic Greek thinkers such as Socrates already knew that politics does not require special knowledge to begin with. Nobody knows better than yourself what is good for you, after all. In his discussion with the sophist Protagoras, Socrates is reported to have argued:

When they've got to come to some general decision on how our city should be run, then anyone at all can get up and give an opinion—he could be a carpenter or a smith; a shoemaker, a shopkeeper or a shipowner; he could be rich or poor; an aristocrat or a nobody. (Plato, 2005: 18)

Democratic decision-making requires engagement and broad participation, not special knowledge. What it does require is practical knowledge—but we have erected systems where practical political knowledge is systematically held back from the people and concentrated in political elites.

In most contemporary democratic political systems, politicians are supposed to exercise a sort of benign tutelage of public things for the people they represent, but instead many of them take actions that serve themselves first and foremost. Many seem willing to sacrifice the very survival of the planet for their own short-term gain and their reelection.

THE ROLE OF SCIENCE AND THE MEDIA

Specialists, that is academics of the social and human sciences as well as those conducting research on climate change and related issues, seem either unable to produce the kind of knowledge that points to viable solutions—or their findings are ignored.

All the while, and certainly connected to this state of affairs, media manipulation has reached new heights. In the United States, but also in many European, Latin American, and Asian countries, irrational politics prevail over sound judgment. War is glorified while the images of war remain hidden from the public. Meat consumption among the affluent has reached new heights, putting further strain on the planet, while the images of mass slaughter of animals remain hidden from the public eye. Cars are getting faster and more powerful every year, while we spend more and more of our time stuck in traffic jams. Fear of others and immigrants is fanned by the media and by politicians in order to justify right-wing political measures and to sell more guns—even if research points to easy access to guns as one of the main causes for the exorbitant homicide rates in such countries as the United States. Many people have radical opinions about others without ever getting a chance, or bothering, to actually know them.

Slowly but surely, as average people are losing their practical knowledge of how democracy works and the kinds of virtues it requires, namely listening and respecting the opinions of others, tolerance, and willingness to compromise. Extremism and conspiracy theories flourish, fanned by professional politicians who use it to justify their autocratic rule and facilitated by a media that lends itself to elevating only the most outrageous opinions. The outgrowths of this tendency are all too familiar. Greta Thunberg, the young Swedish environmental activists and some of her even younger friends and co-activists have received death threats from angry and hateful adults, whose rage is fanned by the media and whose radicalism can blossom to such heights precisely because they lack any sort of practical experience and active involvement in politics and in democracy.

The anonymity provided by the Internet has also provided a platform for the most despicable ideas and opinions. Opinions that could not withstand public debate and scrutiny are thus promoted and spread. Alienation from politics, privatization, and a politics and media culture of hyping up even the smallest incidents is driving a culture of mutual distrust, fear, rage, and suspicion and it has thoroughly undermined communal life. We are slowly but surely losing our common ground, our common sense, and our sense of community.

The arrest of two 6-year-old school children in Orlando in September 2019 highlights this culture of exaggerated reaction vis-à-vis each other. According to the FBI, since 2013, 30,000 children under the age of 10 were arrested in the United States (https://abcnews.go.com/US/30000-children-age-10-arrested-us-2013-fbi/story?id=65798787). Care and mutual responsibility have given way to mutual suspicion, the exaggeration of differences over communalities, and outright manipulation. After all, it is cheap to be radical when one's radicalism does not have to withstand any sort of practical trial or application. Hating those one never meets or faces is a cheap and easy way to vent one's own frustrations and sense of helplessness—particularly when they are children.

In short, our world is out of bounds in many ways, some of which threaten our very survival as a species, while others expose us to the power games of professional politicians, pollsters, media moguls, and multinational corporations.

The promises of democracy and of markets have become hollowed out by political and economic elites who control public affairs and markets, tilting them to their own advantage and favor, apparently willing the sacrifice our communal well-being and the planet's long-term survival over their short-term gains.

This book argues that all these problems are related and that the root cause for all of them lies in the extremely wide gap separating rulers from ruled, or political elites from ordinary people. In most countries of the planet, professional politicians have become a political class for themselves, acting mostly out of self-interest. Even where professional politicians are genuinely invested in working for the public, they do so mostly *for* the public, not *with* it. As a result, politicians have become professionals in political things and average people have become more and more politically ignorant. As such, they have become easy prey of manipulative power holders and the media outlets they control. After all, without a practical understanding of how politics work, extremism becomes an easy and attractive option, as extremism tends to offer simple answers to complex problems. A rising level of political frustration with "the establishment," "the system," or simply with the way thing now work has brought us protest votes, voting abstention, political withdrawal—as well as extremism, nasty anti-politics, xenophobia, and terrorism.

Terrorism, the way I understand it, is simply the last answer to a situation of feeling powerless, frustrated, overlooked, mistreated, misrepresented, and manipulated. Given our current political realities, we should thus not be surprised that terrorism is on the rise everywhere.

CONCLUSION

This book advocates for profound changes in the ways democracies and economies should be governed. It is written for nonacademic readers—all those frustrated with the current status quo but trapped in a situation that seems hopeless and without a viable solution. We are all made to believe that "there are no alternatives" as Margaret Thatcher once argued, and that, in the words of Winston Churchill, "Democracy is the worst form of Government except all those other forms that have been tried from time to time."

In this book, I forcefully argue that there *are* alternatives and that better ways to organize our democracies and markets exist. To see them, we simply need to let go of the old paradigm of liberal, representative democracy, capitalism, or socialism as our only options. New paradigms allow us all to see things afresh.

At the most basic levels, the proposals and solutions I advance and elaborate in this book all dwell on the principle of stakeholdership. This principle states that it is democratically illegitimate to make decision for others. It requires that if you want to decide on issues affecting a broader public, you must have something at stake in it. If you never attended public school and if you do not have your own children attending public school, you cannot legitimately make decisions over public education. If you never took a public bus in your life, you cannot serve as a secretary of public transportation. If you never went to war and none of your family is on active duty, you cannot, legitimately, declare war.

Beyond applying the principle of stakeholdership, I propose *legal duty*, inspired by jury duty, so that average citizens, randomly selected, are actively involved in the making of laws. Coupled with direct democratic politics at the local level, legal duty at the national, transnational, and international level promises to bring our democracies back under the control of average people.

I also propose the establishment of *upper limits* to income and wealth accumulation in order to rein in extreme inequalities, avoid ecological collapse, and establish the conditions for fairness and equal opportunity. Upper limits promise to rein in rampant economic expansion and coupled with other measures, I will discuss in detail later, are likely to lead to a more environmentally sustainable model of economic activity. Fairness and equal opportunity further require, as I will show, a system of *predistribution and reparations* for all those who have been historically excluded from the accumulation of different capitals: financial, educational, residential, cultural, social, racial, and gendered—so all of us can have a fair chance in the different competitive markets we all enter during our lives. Fairness and equal opportunity demand that different people and groups win in competitive markets at different times. That is very different from our current scenario, where some people and some groups always win while others have become systematic losers. It also demands shared responsibilities toward each other and a shift away from emphasizing rights only toward rights and mutual responsibilities.

On the long run, thinking differently about politics and markets requires a rethinking of the state, or maybe, a democratization of the state and a reining in of state power. Today, political and economic elites control our states. In a true democracy, however, the people *are* the state and state sovereignty rests with them.

To get there, we need to "turn our gaze around"—away from the poor and from minorities as those causing us problems and toward the rich and the elites. We need to be willing to rethink what democracy truly means and question those policies that have so firmly been associated with it, such as welfare, minimum salaries, and taxes. If we adopt a different paradigm, call it an "upside down" view, we will see that while minimum wages can be important tools, maximum wages and wealth are far more important for achieving social justice. We will also be able to see that while welfare policies have been important, they are also severely limited. Instead of redistribution, we need to start thinking about predistribution and reparations. And we will have to accept that overconsumption by the affluent is the main problem causing environmental degradation and that our collective survival demands putting a stop to boundless economic growth and expansion.

This book, however, is not about problems. It is about solutions. In what follows, I will thus present and elaborate the solutions a changed optic can produce.

CHAPTER 2

DIRECT LOCAL DEMOCRACY AND LEGAL DUTY

Representative government and trial by jury are the heart and lungs of liberty. Without them we have no fortification against being ridden like horses, fleeced like sheep, worked like cattle, and fed and clothed like swine and hogs.
—John Adams

John Adams, quoted above, similar to all the other founding fathers, was scared of true democracy, referring to it as "mob rule." To him, as well as to his colleagues, people power had to be tempered with all sorts of mechanisms that allow a few, "wise" men like himself, to counterbalance the potentially strong, emotional, and shifting opinions of ordinary men and women. Institutional checks were also required. Checks and balances, separation of powers, and the Electoral College were all designed to hold the direct political influence of ordinary citizens at bay.

John Adams was less concerned about the right of a people to exercise justice over its peers, a system that, as a lawyer, he was well familiar with. As the legitimacy of the Electoral College is being challenged and many of the governmental balances of power are being threatened or outright undermined, it is high time to question the legitimacy of the idea that average people cannot rule themselves. If nothing else, educational levels have risen significantly since Adam's times, when less than 10 percent of all Americans had a high school diploma and over 20 percent of the entire population was illiterate (almost all African Americans were illiterate and excluded from having any political rights—along with women and the poor). But illiteracy is by no means a barrier to political participation, as politics does not require any sort of special knowledge and relies on practical knowledge alone—an insight already voiced by Plato and Socrates in the fifth century BCE.

The purpose of this chapter is to introduce local direct democracy and Legal Duty as a model for informed decision-making by randomly selected average citizens. Legal Duty is inspired by the American jury duty system. Jury duty impacts all participants in important ways, teaching them lessons about what it really means to be a citizen. Because of the random selection of the pool of jurors, American juries are not staffed by elites. There is no campaigning, no voter fraud, and no media distortion affecting the selection of the juror pools—even if bias and discrimination can sneak in at the ultimate selection of jurors, exercised by legal professionals who, again, claim superior knowledge and act as elites within the judicial system.

The core mechanisms securing this lack of distortion is random selection of average citizens. The core exercise leading to civic learning as a juror is deliberation. This chapter will thus hone in on those two important factors: the advantages of random selection and deliberation over voting and the viability of local direct democracy.

The guiding principle that unites direct democracy with legal duty is the principle of stakeholdership, that is, the idea that those, and only those, who have something at stake can and should be involved in the decision-making about a given issue. In other words, following this democratic principle demands that decision should not be made for others. Applying such a principle leads to demanding the active involvement of citizens in the political decision-making affecting them. This principle also helps clarify the decision-making authority of those in power, as for them, too, the same principle holds: they should not make decisions if they are not affected by them.

In this chapter, I will first explore the involvement of citizens in political decision-making through direct democracy at the local level, coupled with legal duty at the regional, state, federal, and even transnational and international levels. I will then also apply the same principle of stakegholdership to elected officials, such as senators.

INSPIRATIONS FROM INDIGENOUS PEOPLE AND ANARCHISM

Direct and council democracy has been a reality among several anarchist communities. It was a practice during the short-lived days of the Paris Commune, in 1871, in Germany in 1918–19, and again in Spain in 1936–37. All three cases offer valuable lessons, which I have already discussed elsewhere

(Reiter, 2019). It is, however, worth repeating the main insights we can gain from analyzing these three cases:

The absence of a uniting ideology, able to provide orientation when it came to favoring one policy over another created much attrition among Paris Commune. So did its convoluted administrative apparatus. Instead of replacing old administrative structures with new ones, the Commune added new structures on top of the old ones, thus doubling the bureaucracy. The protection of private property ensured the continuity of business as usual during the Commune—but is also did not alter the power structures of the city and the country.

Creating a libertarian, decentralized utopia while under siege from foreign nations and the own, French army, it turns out, is not a practical route towards a better future, as the state represents and controls violence, but the Commune, while able in theory to assemble and organize power, diluted it, thus becoming vulnerable to the onslaught of concentrated and organized violence. The artisan socialism of anarchist and libertarian bent that was erected in Paris in 1871 was thus doomed from the beginning, as it faced concentrated and hierarchically organized state-led military violence.

During the short-lived German Räte Republic, local council republics were enacted, taking advantage of the power vacuum created after WWI. They did not last long and were unable to erect a system structured according to their believes. External threats were constant—from rightwing conservatives and from the dogmatic, socialist left, which ultimately undermined the anarchists. While they lasted, the German councils had a shared vision and guidance (even if not religious, but very spirited) from their different leaders. They strongly felt that they had to take matters into their own hands and thus participated actively and strongly.

The core proposal of this movement was self-organization of workers and soldiers, mostly at the fabric level. In practice, the German revolution never eliminated the parliamentary system, despite the critique of some of its core anarchist proponents. However, core to the idea of the council republic was (and is) the imperative mandate, that is: parliamentary deputies can only enact policies in accordance with concretely transmitted preference by their electors.

As explained above, the five principles of the council idea, according to Ernst Däuming (1920) are: 1. Proletarians, not citizens, as actors;

2. Anti-capitalism; 3. Anti-parliamentarism; 4. No long-term powers to delegates and permanent possibility of instant recall; 5. Anti-political party (proletariat as a whole).

Core is also the idea espoused by Gustav Landauer, namely of direct, local participation in the legislative process. "Each republic must be sovereign and based on participatory democracy, strong municipal autonomy, and cooperatives. The current workers', soldiers', and peasants' councils are the right beginning." (Gustav Landauer, November 1918, in Kuhn, 2012: 175f)

Political parties have no place in a council republic. Erich Mühsam warned against them repeatedly: "I feared that forming a party would have the same consequences it had always had in Germany: the submission of the proletarian revolutionary will to party interests." (Erich Mühsam, 1920, in Kuhn, 2012: 216)

Finally, state bureaucracies must be changed if a community seeks to change the way power is brokered and administered. The failure to do so was probably the main cause for the demise of the German Council Republics.

During the "Anarchist Spring" of Spain, the places where direct democracy worked the best and longest was in rural communities of Aragon and Andalucia—where power vacuums were created by the civil war. Direct democracies were practiced there as long as the absence of external threat allowed for it. They came to an end when the Nationalist troops, let by general Franco, took power. The direct democratic experiments were local and sought to construct a federalist system—but they were unable to achieve this goal. The accounts we have thus stem from local communities, organizing themselves.

Similar to what happened in Germany in 1918, Spanish anarchism was not given much of a chance. It was able to install itself only briefly, but during times of turmoil and war, which made it impossible to execute its core principles. Similar to Germany, councils emerged in Spain spontaneously, as the first response by frustrated workers and farmers who had long suffered from the exploitation of abusive landowners, company owners, and governments. Protest and rage were directed at once against formal state institutions and their representatives, as they represented the oppression from which ordinary people had long suffered.

Once established, collective ownership was among the first measures taken, followed by collective decision-making in open assemblies. Confederation followed. Wages were equalized and work teams were formed. A rational distribution of tasks and a need-based distribution of profits in the form of family-wages were quickly instituted in most places, particularly in the countryside, were anarchism had more time to take root and where it also found more peace to be implemented, lasting for several years in some Aragon and Andaluce municipalities.

It is worth noting here that Spain counts on a long tradition of open assemblies, called "cabildos," which reaches back to the 6th century, after the decay of the Roman Empire in this region. Open cabildos were village assemblies that met to make collective decisions, but particularly to pass laws.

Those parts of Spain controlled by the Anarchists in 1936–37 formed a dual organizational structure, consisting of local trade organizations (*secciones de oficio*), which together formed larger, federal unions for each occupation (*unions de oficio*)—and regional federations, irrespective of the specific trade or occupation (*federaciones locales*). According to Bookchin, "This dual structure forms the bedrock of all syndicalist forms of organization. In Spain, as elsewhere, the structure was knitted together by workers' committees, which originated in individual shops, factories, and agricultural communities. Gathering together in assemblies, the workers elected from their midst the committees that presided over the affairs of the vocational *Secciones de oficio* and the geographic *Federaciones locales*. They were federated into regional committees for nearly every large area of Spain." (Bookchin, 1994: 11)

The kind of liberal anarchism established by Comuneros in Spain emerged during times of war and turmoil, which created a power vacuum, promptly and eagerly filled by peasants and workers. Their decentralized organizations, however, were no match for the onslaught of the fascists under Franco, or even the much more centrally organized communists. Libertarian anarchism is able to provide freedom by abandoning the state, but it cannot resist the onslaught of centralized state and military power. (Reiter, 2019: 114–17)

Historical experiments of liberal anarchists, Owenites, Tolstoyens and others who decided to break away from centralizing state power and control offer valuable lessons about what appears to be our intuitive response to organizing our collective lives, namely collectively and relying on councils of citizens. Similar organizational patterns emerge whenever humans were left to organize themselves—be it in medieval European city-states or among other communities and communes who consciously set themselves apart to live their lives according to their own desires. Hierarchies and the power over others emerge only reluctantly and against the resistance of free people, executed by those who seek to construct states and bureaucracies whose primary aim is to control average people and extract surplus from them. The work of James Scott (2009, 2017) amply testifies to this development—and the resistance of some free people against encroaching states and the control they seek to implement.

It is not surprising that people resist state power, as most of human history was lived in stateless societies. Before the Neolithic revolution, human groups indeed organized in egalitarian groups (Clastres, 1989) and whenever state power breaks down, it is to this form of collective and egalitarian self-organization that humans tend to converge. Most hunter and gatherer societies to this day do not recognize strong hierarchies among them and they resist the leadership, and abuse by one of them, or of a small group, over all others (Turnbull, 1968).

Similarly, valuable lessons can be learned from indigenous communities across Africa and the Americas, most of whom have a long history of practicing direct democracy. Countries such a Botswana have recognized village democracy, *kgotla*, in their constitution. Many Native American people, north and south of the equator, can look back as long histories of egalitarian self-rule before the European conquest—and some of them still practice egalitarian self-rule to this day. I have been able to study the practice of direct and council democracy among the Wintukua of Colombia, commonly known as Arhuacos (Reiter, 2019). The democratic practices of the Zapatistas of southern Mexico have also been widely described and discussed (e.g., by Baronnet, Bayo, and Stahler-Sholk, 2011). The direct democratic experiences of autonomous indigenous villages of Bolivia, as well as the many village democracies existing in different African countries all contain political institutions that have proven successful for the protection of broad, village-based citizen political participation. Bolivia has a population of over 11 million, Switzerland has some 8.5 million, and Vermont some 620,000. While relatively small, these countries and states clearly demonstrate that direct local democracy *can* be a sustained reality as long as they are embedded in decentralized federal political systems.

Considered together, these historical and contemporary empirical examples contain a formidable toolbox for the practice of direct democracy at the local level.

In my own attempt to identify the common ground shared by all these experiences, I found that it takes shared interest to make these democratic experiments viable. This shared interest can be produced by a shared culture, as is the case among indigenous groups; but it can also be produced by shared values and commitments, as the local direct democratic experiences of many intentional and religious communes demonstrate. Once a group of people share the same beliefs and convictions, differences in background, ethnicity and even language can be overcome, as some religious communes, like the Kibbuzim, the Hutterities, or the Amish show. Some intentional communes, like the Twin Oaks Commune in Virginia, have persisted for decades, finding ways to avoid the abuse of some by others and allowing all to be true political beings—zoon politicon.

LAWMAKING AS THE CENTRAL PLACE FOR DEMOCRATIC LEGITIMACY

For French Philosopher Jean-Jacques Rousseau (1712–78), "Law being purely the declaration of the general will, it is clear that, in the exercise of the legislative power, the people cannot be represented" (Rousseau, 2003: 65). According to Rousseau, what makes a republic democratic is not the fact that citizens elect representatives, but rather that citizens themselves make the laws they live under. This task, for Rousseau, cannot be delegated.

Accordingly, the law of a land should emerge from the people, where custom and traditions gradually consolidate and become enshrined in legal codes or in legal precedence. In real democracies, laws and constitutions should thus "travel up" from the people and become consolidated and then enforced. Jürgen Habermas, the German philosopher and social scientist, has argued that for a law to be considered truly democratic and legitimate, all those who fall under it must have had a say, or a voice, in its making (Habermas, 1998). While this sets a very high bar, the idea behind it is very important: in a true democracy, nobody can be made to live under and accept a law that has been enforced from above—without the participation of the citizenry. A democracy demands that all citizens play an active role in lawmaking and laws are only legitimate to the extent that all those affected by it participated in its making. Despotism, on the other hand, is characterized by a situation of one person, or a group thereof, making and enforcing laws of their own making onto others. One of the outcomes of such a situation is, of course, a frequent breaking of the law, or rebellion against it.

Lawmaking, in short, is the core place upon which democratic legitimacy hinges. If we accept this analysis, then the core question for democratic legitimacy is: who makes the laws? Is it the people themselves or is it a group of elites who have either usurped this power or who have been elected to do so as representatives of the people? A true democracy requires that the people living under a body of laws make those laws themselves. As this seems impossible, the question becomes: how to get closest to this ideal?

THE ADVANTAGES OF RANDOM SELECTION OVER VOTING

Elections are the core cause for many of the problems most of our democracies face today. Elections, in our days of intensive media exposure, have created a system where those able to spend the most money on their campaigns have the best chance to win an election. Instead of selecting the best, or most suited among us to do the job at hand, elections have produced a system where we routinely end up with the richest instead—and in many cases also with those with the least scruples to make outrageous statements, able to capture the largest audience. Election have opened the door to manipulation, electoral fraud, exclusion from voting rights, and all sorts of other distortions, all of which effect the democratic process negatively. Even in the best-case scenario, we tend to elect those with the best rhetoric, the strongest charisma, the ones taller than the average, men over women, whites over blacks, Hispanics, or Asians, and people with more hair over those whose baldness seems to indicate, as some unconscious level, a lack of virility.

Elections are, of course, connected to political representation, and political representation is even more at fault for our current democratic problems. Political representation, after all, relies on the idea that some people can conduct politics *for* the rest of us, which, at its very core, is an anti-democratic idea—at least if we understand democracy in its original meaning, as rule of average people. Democracy still carries the promise of self-rule—but political representation systematically undermines this promise by allowing some to rule over others. Political representation has divided any democracy where it is practiced into rulers and ruled, which is precisely the reality against which democracies were first created and institutionalized.

If we have to have people ruling over others then, at least, we need to ensure that all of us can become rulers at one point in our lives and that those ruling over others cannot abuse their power and not rule for long. None of these crucial provisions, all going back to ancient Athens and Republican Rome, are currently being enforced in any real democracy. Political representation coupled with elections has given us a system of elite rule and of political manipulation on a mass scale. The more and the longer we leave political affairs to a few, elected elites, the more we can expect them to carve out ways, rules, and institutions that protect their rule and shield them from the power and oversight of the people. To safe democracy, we need to think about ways on how to curb the power of elites and give voice to average citizens. The old justification that we, as a people, are unable to rule ourselves has become more ludicrous than it ever was in human history.

DELIBERATION

Seyla Benhabib, a prominent American philosopher, argues that "a public sphere of deliberation about matters of mutual concern is essential to the legitimacy of democratic institutions" (Benhabib, 1996: 68). Another prominent scholar, Bernard Manin, already wrote in 1987:

> It is, therefore, necessary to alter radically the perspective common to both liberal theories and democratic thought: the source of legitimacy is not the predetermined will of individuals, but rather the process of its formation, that is, deliberation itself. An individual's liberty consists first of all in being able to arrive at a decision by a process of research and comparison among various solutions. As political decisions are characteristically imposed on all, it seems reasonable to seek, as an essential condition for legitimacy, the deliberation of all or, more precisely, the right of all to participate in deliberation. (Manin, 1987: 351f)

There are several arguments for deliberation: First, deliberation assures legitimacy. Second, deliberation leads to more informed decisions, as information is shared in dialogue and different perspectives are taken into account and interchanged. Third, through deliberation, individual preferences become more reasonable and ordered, as preferences cannot be thought of as given, but rather as the result of dialogue. Fourth, the publicity and reflexivity of public discourse allows for a constant redefining and questioning of what is perceived as "good" and "right," which is particularly important under conditions of modernity, characterized by a plurality of worldviews. Exposing one's opinion to a broader public also offers the possibility of sorting out anti-democratic arguments, as these arguments are likely to be challenged. Furthermore, deliberation promises individual learning.

Despite its weaknesses, potential pitfalls, and its fragility to fall prey to sophists and manipulators, deliberation still is our only legitimately democratic way on how to reach collective decisions. For deliberation to work properly, some conditions need to be met and upheld:

First equality and symmetry of the participants must be assured. All must have the same chance to speak and be heard. All must have the same right to question the agenda setting. All participants must have the right to challenge the procedural rules that organize the discussion, as well as the agendas of what will be discussed. There can be no fixed rules that limit the agenda and exclude certain topics. All individuals that are potentially affected by a decision must be able to participate in the process of decision-making. Most importantly, the outcomes of deliberations must not be unanimous. Differences must be allowed to prevail and persist. If binding decisions have to be made, then deliberations can either end in a vote or they must allow room for dissent. The protection of minority opinions becomes an important ingredient to avoid that deliberations lead to totalitarian outcomes.

Deliberation also has upper limits with regard to the number of people who can deliberate together. The research conducted by Frank Bryan and his colleagues about town halls in Vermont allow us to gage this reality and establish some upper limits for meaningful deliberation. According to Clark and Bryan, who have researched participation in town halls conducted yearly in Vermont: "Town meetings work better, dramatically better, in towns with small populations. Towns like Waltham, Grafton, Sandgate, Belvidere, Roxbury and Wheelock (all with fewer than 600 voters on the checklist) average 30 percent attendance at town meeting, while towns like Middlebury, Bennington, Hartford, Waterbury and Swanton (all with more than 3,600 voters on the checklist) average about 5 percent" (Clark and Bryan, 2005: 40).

Analyzing data gathered from 1,435 town meetings, selected randomly from 1970 to 1998 in Vermont, Frank Bryan is able to show that the smaller the town, the higher the percentage of citizens participating in town meetings and the more likely they are to speak at the event. Bryan combines these two indicators into one, calling it "democraticness." Democraticness measures the percentage of registered voters attending a town meeting and actually saying something there, that is, it measures active participation or active citizenship. He finds that "for every increase of one rank of its population size, a town's town meeting will lose about nine-tenths (0.88) of a rank in 'democraticness'" (Bryan, 2004: 18). He concludes:

> In the description of the towns one condition overwhelms: their size. By nearly every standard a political scientist might employ, they are tiny. One-quarter of the meetings were held in towns that averaged fewer than 1,000 residents. Of the 1,435 meetings, 113 were held in towns that averaged fewer than 200. Only 2 percent of the meetings were held in towns of more than 5,000. (Bryan, 2004: 20)

Indeed, Bryan found that "about 42 percent of the variance in attendance at the 1,435 town meetings is associated with the size of the town where the meeting is held" (Bryan, 2004: 73). The relative power to influence collective decisions, another measure of size, explains some 58 percent of the variance.

Among the large sample Bryan assembled, participation in town meetings dropped off at around one thousand registered voters. In some of the smaller towns, attendance was as high as 74 percent, whereas in the larger towns (3,500 registered voters and above), attendance dropped as low as 1 percent. The same research also found that "in general town meetings with the smallest number of people in attendance have the largest percentage of participators and the best distribution of participation among those present" (Bryan, 2004: 157).

While Bryan does not give a precise upper limit for meaningful direct democracy based on direct personal interaction, his numbers closely resemble those proposed by Robin Dunbar, who has asserted that the human brain is only able to maintain 150 stable relationships, thus forming the upper limit of stable, cohesive groups (Dunbar, 1992). Dunbar, in fact, argues that "when a group's size exceeds this limit, it becomes unstable and begins to fragment. This then places an upper limit on the size of groups which any given species can maintain as cohesive social units through time" (Dunbar, 1992: 469).

Upper limits to the viability of direct democracy thus creates a problem for the kinds of solutions I am proposing here. However, this problem is not unsurmountable, and it simply is not true that direct democracy cannot work, for pragmatic reasons, in large and complex democracies. What becomes clear from the work of Frank Bryan and others is that direct democracy at the local level must be part of the solution toward invigorated democracies. This work shows that direct democracy is possible at the local level and has been a reality in many places and countries. Vermont and those Swiss cantons still practicing direct democracy, Glarus and Appenzell Innerrhoden, along with many historical examples, intentional and religious communes, and many native and indigenous communities across the globe contain the recipes and institutional knowledge to make local direct democracy possible. All we need to do is learn from them and apply the many lessons they can teach us to those formal democracies relying exclusively on voting and elite rule. What is also clear from the available literature and experience is that democratic self-rule in the form of local direct democracy with the participation of all must rely on decentralization and a system of federalism, or even confederation, allowing local communities to make decisions about their own lives locally.

Legitimate laws must emerge locally and be crafted and decided by local communities. But what about national, or even international decision and lawmaking?

WHAT WE CAN LEARN FROM JURY DUTY

Jury trials have a long tradition in the world. Being judged by a group of one's peers and community members must be seen as the original way groups of people dealt with crime and the breaking of the norms and rules of a society before one person or a group of people were able to usurp power and establish monarchies, aristocracies, or any other form of elite rule through state power. We know about jury trials in ancient Athens and in Republican Rome and even in Greek myth, referenced by such authors as Aeschylus. Hunter and gatherer, also known as foraging societies, to this day confront crime and transgression of societal norms collectively, in most cases through the participation of all members of the affected group. Many indigenous societies of the Americas do the same.

In democratic Athens, jury trials counted on hundreds of randomly selected members and a special council, called *nomothetai*, existed to evaluate legislative proposals made by the citizen assembly at large (*ekklesia*) and proposed by the council of 500.

Jury trials were central to such foundational documents as the Magna Carta (1215) and we know of jury trials playing an important role among the Vikings, in Medieval Europe, and in the Muslim World.

Different forms of jury trials are a reality today in such countries as the United Kingdom, Norway, Argentina, Japan, Greece, Canada, Italy, parts of Switzerland, Ireland, Belgium, Australia, Austria, France, New Zealand, Russia, India, and the United States.

In the United States, the right to be judged by a jury of one's peers is mentioned in the American Declaration of Independence, in the American Constitution, and in the Bill of Rights—the first 10 Amendments to the American Constitution. In the United States, jury pools are randomly selected among all US citizens, based on voter registration and driver license records. In criminal cases, a jury of 12 jurors deliberates, in private, about the facts of the crime until it reaches a guilty or non-guilty verdict, where most states require a unanimous vote among the jurors to issue a verdict. Jurors on federal court cases are compensated with a stipend of $50 per day. Most jury duties last only a few days.

Political scientists have long argued that participation in a jury has important effects on the participants and on American democracy. Alexis de Tocqueville, who travelled the United States in 1835, argued that jury duty taught American citizens important virtues and was thus central to American democracy. In a recent study, John Gastil, Pierre Dees, Philip Weiser, and Cindy Simmons (2010) found prove that participation in a jury impacted the jurors in such a way that they became more politically aware and active. Many jurors who did not vote before started voting after having served in a jury and many started reading the news more than they did before. Overall, the research these authors conducted clearly demonstrates that citizens, after having served on a jury, became more involved in civic and political activities in general.

LEGAL DUTY

James Fishkin (2018), in his conducting of deliberative polls, has been able to involve hundreds of people in collective lawmaking. He simply reduces the number of deliberators by breaking up larger groups into deliberative tables of up to 15 participants. Each table has one person who ensures that all can speak, and no distortions occur. The same person then reports to the larger group the conclusions or recommendations the table has reached. By proceeding this way, even very large groups can deliberate.

Fishkin's work offers another important insight. If we accept the principle of stakeholdership and that deliberation and the making of laws are the necessary core ingredients of self-rule and democracy and that sortition is more democratic than election, then we must find a way how to involve ordinary, average citizens in the process of proposing, debating, and passing of laws. This can best be achieved through stratified random sampling, to ensure that all those potentially affected by a law are represented in its crafting.

Jury duty can serve as an example for the realm of the law. Most American citizens only serve on a jury once or twice during their lives, given the average of some 1.5 million citizens serving as jurors per year and a total adult population of some 250 million.

Legal duty would call on citizens and residents of the place for which a new law is proposed to meet and deliberate about the merits of the proposal. If new laws are proposed at the city level, then only those living in the city in question would need to be in the pool from which legal deliberators are selected. If it is a state law, then the pool must include the citizens and residents of that state—and if a national law is proposed, a national pool of legal deliberators must be created. In bearing with the lessons learned from such experiences, the total number of deliberators, even if broken down into tables of 15, should probably not exceed 200—even if Fishkin and his team were able to conduct deliberative polls with up to 300 people.

Polls must be stratified in such a way to represent the population of a new bill or legal proposal so that all potentially affected populations and groups are represented in the group of deliberators. Stratified samples must thus take account of race, gender, age, and class. This could mean that if a law is proposed for a city with a higher than average percentage of elderly, the elderly must also be overrepresented among deliberators. The same is true for minorities, alien residents, Latinxs, African Americans, Asians, people with different disabilities, and so on as already argued above. Democracy also requires that young adults aged 16 and older participate in such deliberations, as they, too, will be affected by a law. Particularly for them, participation in legal deliberations must be seen as an important component of democratic training and socialization.

Legal deliberators must be given notice that they need to report to a specified place to debate the bill or bills at hand. Free public transportation should be provided to all legal deliberators, as Switzerland does, and deliberators should be compensated for their public service the same way federal jurists are currently compensated in the United States. Legal deliberations should be preceded by publicly available information on the proposed bills—similar to the ways some direct democratic Swiss cantons currently make the agenda and relevant background information for collective decisions available in advance.

Deliberations should not last longer than three days. Once larger groups are broken down to tables of up to 15 and once we have stratified samples of deliberators representing all those affected by a new law—we can scale up local direct democracy by adding sortition to it at the regional, national, and even international levels. At the end of the deliberative process, the deliberators need to vote in favor or against a proposed law. They should also be able to amend any bills, thus reflecting potential learning and changing of opinion that has occurred during deliberations. Once the deliberators voted, their decisions must be binding and become law—without having to go through elected officials. However, as long as there exists another branch of congress, deliberators, instead of making a final decision on a bill, could pass their decision on to the Senate and the president for signature, thus following currently established procedure.

THE HOUSE OF DELIBERATION

While sortition is superior in its ability to secure and protect democracy to election, for practical reasons I propose a gradual substitution of elected officials with citizen deliberators. In a first step, in countries with bicameral political systems like the United States, the current House of Representatives should be replaced with a House of Deliberation, while maintaining a reformed Senate and executive branch, at least until more practical knowledge and experience with the House of Deliberation has been accumulated, allowing for its fine tuning and adjustment, where necessary.

Ideally, there should be a House of Deliberation at the national, state, and city levels, potentially also at county levels, allowing for the deliberation of regional ordinances and proposals. Within such entities as the European Union, a European House of Deliberation should substitute the current Parliament. Even internationally, we can think about a United Nations relying on randomly drawn citizens from across the globe, coming together to deliberate world issues whenever needed and called upon.

Legal deliberations could be supported by deliberative polls, the way James Fishkin and his team already conduct. Deliberative polls should be employed for extraordinary decisions such as the rewriting or amendment to a constitution, specific city or regional plans, or to determine the budget so that legal duty could be reserved to stricter legislative purposes.

BUDGETING

Budgeting, as has become clear in such countries as the United States over the past years, has fallen victim to the political hackling of elected officials. Politicians, including the president, have routinely used budgeting as a tool to push their political agendas. The federal budgeting process in the United States provides probably the clearest example of how the people are held hostage by elected officials who are effectively reversing popular sovereignty in this process.

Budgeting, as the over thousand empirical examples worldwide of "participatory budgeting" (PB) have demonstrated, can be done effectively by the people themselves. Most current examples of participatory budgeting follow the model established in Porto Alegre, Brazil, where PB was first created in the 1980s. From there, it spread across Brazil and the globe, promoted by the World Bank and other international agencies. Today, some 1,500 cities have implemented this policy (www.participatorybudgeting.org). According to the *Participatory Budgeting Project*, an American nonprofit organization whose mission is to "empower people to decide together how to spend public money,

> Participatory budgeting (PB) is a different way to manage public money, and to engage people in government. It is a democratic process in which community members directly decide how to spend part of a public budget. It enables taxpayers to work with government to make the budget decisions that affect their lives. (www.participatorybudgeting.org)

In Porto Alegre, the municipal government organized biyearly assemblies to inform the citizenry. Delegates and councilors were representing regions. In addition, PB contained a quota system, based on the level of popular mobilization; the strategic importance of the region for Porto Alegre; the population in needy areas; and infrastructure deficiency. Almost 65 percent of revenues were allocated to the five top-rated regions. Participation under this model steadily grew with an average of 6,000 participants in the public meetings. In 1993, the administration created thematic forums for transportation and circulation; urban planning and the organization of the city; education and culture; health and social assistance; and economic development and tax reform. According to analyst Rebecca Abers, "Like the regional assemblies, the second round of thematic assemblies elected two members and two alternates to the Municipal Budget Council, giving that group forty-two voting members" (Abers, 2000: 85). In an effort to explain why PB was able to mobilize poor citizens, living in underserved neighborhoods, Abers finds that PB "effectively reduced the costs and increased the perceived benefits of participation in several ways" (Abers, 2000: 135).

However, after its bureaucratization in 2004, PB in Porto Alegre lost much of its appeal and vitality and neighborhood associations have largely withdrawn from the process. With the withdrawal of the mayor and his secretaries and the cutting back of the decidable budget, PB has lost much of its importance and verve and participation waned in its birthplace, Porto Alegre.

Still, participatory budgeting can teach us a few important lessons on citizen participation and direct democratic decision-making. First and foremost, budgeting can be done by the people and does not need to be done exclusively by elected official or experts. Second, average people will participate in collective decision-making assemblies as long as there is something real and concrete to decide. Third, once people decide, handing those decision over to elected officials undermines the legitimacy of the whole process and undermines participation. And fourth, large, multilayered assemblies who elect representatives to higher up assemblies is not the way to go, as it demands too much time, too much organization, and involves too many people at the same time, making meaningful deliberation impossible and creating logistic nightmares.

Legal duty, in contrast, would rely on smaller groups of citizens, even if federal budget decisions should involve a larger sample of citizens—maybe 200. If selected, citizens and residents would need to receive the required information to be able to make informed decisions about how the federal budget should be spent. They should be supported by professional bureaucrats who must provide expert opinions and offer advice. The decision about how the federal budget should be spent should rest, however, with the deliberators.

THE SENATE AND THE PRESIDENT

My initial proposal to invigorate and democratize democracy foresees for bicameral countries like the United States that only the House of Representative be replaced by a House of Deliberation. Once such a mixed system has taken root, allowing for its adjustment and refinement, it remains an option to also transform the upper house or Senate into a deliberative entity.

For now, however, the democratization of democracy and the application of the principle of stakeholdership demands that the Senate also undergoes reform in order to avoid its growing distance from the citizenry. To rein in the abuse of power by many senators, strict one-term limits would need to be imposed, thus counteracting the tendency of senators to become professional politicians and to avoid the great emphasis currently placed on winning reelection.

Campaign contribution must be altogether outlawed and each candidate running for a Senate seat must be given equal airtime on public radio and TV stations in the weeks leading up to an election. Brazil is already practicing such a design and its experience can inform other countries. There, any candidate passing a minimum threshold of public support is given the same amount of media airtime. Such a system avoids the US scenario where elections are currently won by those willing or able to spend the most money on their political campaigns. External lobbying and campaign financing by powerful individuals and corporations is thereby also avoided, while the enforcement of a minimum threshold ensures that not all self-declared candidates receive free airtime. The electoral council must be reformed or abolished, and the indirect election of the president made direct.

Lawrence Lessig (2019) has explained in detail what is needed to reform the electoral process of senators. The same rule he elaborates must apply to the election of the president. Beyond Lessig's recommendations, my proposal of thinking about politics in terms of direct participation and stakeholding further suggests that senators must be held publicly accountable after they step down from public office, as they used to do during the Roman Republic.

Furthermore, we, as a people, should not allow candidates to run for public office who do not believe in the merits of public office holding, as is the case of so many candidates today. The guiding principle here is also inspired by the idea of direct participation, active stakeholding, and the absence of delegation: if you don't believe in public service, then you are barred from running for public office. The application of this principle produces some other, surprising, insights: If you want to manage public education, you must also use it and you should not be allowed to send your children to private schools. If you want to make decisions about war, you must have a stake in it in the form of your kin serving in it. It is time to end decision-making for others and over others without having a stake in it. We are all ill served by ministers and secretaries of public transportation who never took a public bus and we are better served by politicians or bureaucrats responsible for public health who are actively involved in public health provision.

Other insights about elected officials and career bureaucrats might grow out of rethinking them in terms of direct participation, stakeholdership, delegation, and public control. These are important to consider, as we might one day decide to get rid altogether of professional lawmakers, senators included, but we will most likely always have to rely on professional bureaucrats to administer our collective affairs, after we collectively decided what to do. While this book is dedicated to rethinking political representation and capitalism, a broader rethinking of rule also demands a rethinking of bureaucracies. This is, however, not a task I can tackle here.

CITIZEN RESPONSIBILITY

One of the core convictions advocated in this book is that democracy requires active citizen participation and involvement. The liberal ideal that ordinary citizens can simply leave politics and public affairs to a group of elites while pursuing their own private interests is, in my assessment, dead. It has brought us massive abuse, manipulation, misinformation, extremism, political apathy, cynicism, and withdrawal from politics. If we want democracy, we must be willing to do something for it—even if our involvement is minimal and reduced to doing jury and legal services once or twice in our lifetimes. Sortition could be controlled in such a way that nobody is required to serve more than once every five years, thus keeping public involvement very manageable for citizens and residents. At the same time, abstaining from politics should not be an option. Rights, after all, have to be upheld by collective responsibilities and duties. One of the problems our current democracies face is that some people and groups have lots of rights without any responsibilities or duties toward the very collective that ensures those rights. For them, rights have become entitlements, free of any obligations and responsibilities toward their fellow citizens. Others, on the other hand, have many obligations, but very few rights. In a democracy, rights and responsibilities must go hand in hand. In a democracy, there are no entitlements to having rights without contributing to their upholding and their enforcement.

Today, 27 countries on this planet have compulsory voting. They recognize and enforce that reaping the benefits of living in a democracy demands active political participation. Again, reaping the benefits while not contributing is an aristocratic, not a democratic, practice and should not be allowed in a democracy.

This means for jury and legal duty that those randomly selected must comply—even if exception and accommodations should be allowed in the case of sickness, undue hardship resulting from deliberative participation, or prearranged travel. At the same time, compulsory participation in the election of the Senate and the president should be enforced and nonparticipation sanctioned.

LEGAL INITIATIVE

Legal initiatives, plebiscites, and participatory budgeting and planning are already a reality in many countries, states, and cities, thus pointing to other, complementary institutional designs that allow for more democratic ways of a people to govern themselves. For legal duty to work, legal initiatives would assume a much more central place in politics, as the central way to propose new laws. Bills could still be proposed by the members of the Senate or upper house, but the more democratic way to proceed is to leave the proposal of new laws to popular initiatives along the lines already practiced in California or Switzerland, thus requiring a minimum amount of signatures to initiate a legal initiative and trigger the assembly of deliberators. To limit the power and influence of professional "signature gatherers," the threshold for proposing new laws should be set low enough so that average citizens can have a fair chance to propose a legal initiative (see Fishkin, 2018 for a discussion of this issue).

Plebiscites should also play an integral part of a true democracy—and here as well we can simply follow the examples already established, and practiced in such places as California and Switzerland, with the necessary adjustments so that the power and influence of rich people, able to buy professional "signature gatherers," can be counterbalanced and controlled.

SCALING UP: DIRECT DEMOCRACY IN LARGE DEMOCRACIES

Most skeptics of direct democracy either argue that it is impossible to practice in large, modern societies or that it is undesirable, potentially leading to a "Balkanization of politics" and the exclusion of minorities. Both of these arguments are wrong.

The argument that direct democracy necessarily leads to balkanization, division, and the exclusion of minorities relies on an old paradigm, which associates democracy with the nation-state and the impossibility of border crossing. It is certainly true that direct democracy and deliberation put all those who do not agree with the majority under stress—but provisions to protect dissenters and minorities are certainly not reserved to representative democracies and must be enacted and upheld in direct democratic systems.

Furthermore, we need to start thinking about belonging to a democratic community beyond the current ways regulating citizenship and nationhood. It is, in fact, a morally unsustainable and highly undemocratic practice to regulate access to rights and privileges not by effort or merit—but by birthplace and/or by the nationality of the biological father. *Jus soli* and *jus sanguinis*, the regulation of citizenship by birthplace or by descent, are today's only ways of regulating access to right and privileges, but they are not democratic. *Jus soli* and *jus sanguinis* are instead colonial impositions on the world, forced onto the countries of the Global South by their colonial overlords. Under these regimes, having rights equals winning a "birth lottery" by simply being born in the "right" place. All those born in Africa, Latin America, most of the Caribbean, and great parts of Asia are simply born in the "wrong" places and suffer different hardships without being responsible for any of them.

Democracy demands free association, so that people or groups not agreeing with the laws and rules of one community can leave that community and choose another, more in line with their own convictions (Ziai, 2019). Protections of dissenters and minorities coupled with the possibility to freely choose the community to which one wants to belong are thus two important provisions for more direct, deliberative democracies, even if utopian, under the current paradigms. A shift from defining democracies exclusively through 'having rights' to 'having mutual obligations and responsibilities' will further weaken the currently dominant system of treating belonging as a birth right.

The myth of deliberative democracy's impracticality is equally easy to dispel. As already explained above, the viability of true democracy relies on a combination of local direct democracy with legal duty at the regional, national, and international levels. Federalism, or even confederation, a stronger form of federalism, must be part of such a system to make it viable. The political scientist James Fishkin has conducted "deliberative polls" in such large countries as Mongolia, with a population of over some 3 million people, many of whom widely dispersed over a vast country. In 2015, some 300 randomly selected Mongolian delegates came together to deliberate about the capital's master plan. Fishkin (2018) has conducted similar deliberative polls in California, Texas, and in Uganda and David van Reybrouck (2018) relates successful experiments with randomly selected deliberative forums in Ireland, Iceland, British Columbia and Ontario (Canada), and the Netherlands. The core element that makes deliberation work at a large scale is the breaking up of large groups into small groups of up to 15 deliberators.

Another core ingredient making deliberation possible on a large scale are stratified random samples. Stratified random sampling involves random selection among the different groups present, or affected, by a policy in order to assure that men and women, the elderly, the middle aged, the young, as well as different ethnic and income groups, are all represented in the deliberating group. The third, important ingredient for successful deliberation is time and access to information. In the deliberative polls Fishkin conducts, people are given two to three days to deliberate and they are provided upfront with the information they require to make informed decisions. The direct democratic cantons of Switzerland proceed the same way, making the agenda of public deliberations available weeks before the event and offering free train tickets on the day of the public assembly.

A recent study conducted by political scientists Michael Neblo, Kevin Esterling, and David Lazer (2018) has shown that average people are very capable of making informed decisions—if they are given the conditions to do so and as long as they have reason to participate in such an exercise.

Scaling up deliberative democracy is thus possible and randomly selected deliberators not only represent "the people" in a much better and clearer way, but their random selection also shields the whole system from all of the problems voting produces: fraud, manipulation, lobbying, undue influence of money, and so on. Just imagine a democracy where instead of elected politicians, randomly selected average citizens were to make decision about how to spend the country's budget, which laws to enact, or which countries to invade, if any.

CONCLUSION

The last decades and centuries of democratic history have shown that democracy requires active participation. Democracy cannot be delegated to a group of supposed specialists. The opposite also holds: if you want to make decisions for us, you must have a stake in the thematic field for which you decide. Politics does not require special knowledge and professional politicians are not specialists to begin with. All they achieve is to shield average citizens from actively learning about politics through applied practice.

The central and most important component of this proposal consists of substituting elected lawmakers with randomly selected average citizens who are given the time and the information required to deliberate about a new law or the revision of an old one. Legal duty, combined with local direct democracy, participatory budgeting, deliberative polls, public initiatives, and plebiscites must be the way we govern ourselves in the future, once we accept the new paradigm, which states that in a true democracy average people need to rule themselves by actively participating in the crafting of those laws that affect them. The core ingredient of democracy thus is direct democracy at the local level in a federal system. Beyond the local level, the principle of stakeholdership demands sortition over election and the active involvement of those making decisions in the domains they decide about.

If randomly selected citizen representatives were to make political decisions instead of elected politicians, we would avoid most of the problems we currently face. Because there is not enough research into this possibility, there is not enough debate about how many people should actively participate in such a process, for how long they should deliberate, when they should vote at the end of deliberation, and how much compensation they should receive in return for the public service. However, studying and trying out of different formulas is what we require if we want to move beyond the current crisis of democracy.

Deliberative polls have proven to work for reaching informed policy decision, as well as to redraft constitutions, as the case of Iceland clearly demonstrates. However, deliberative polls to this day have only produced recommendations, which were then submitted to elected officials. Deliberative polls work, but they are not the only mechanisms we need to move away from democratic crisis and to further democratize our existing democracies. To achieve that goal, deliberative polls need to be supported by legal duty and direct citizen involvement at the local level, where it is viable.

My proposal thus requires federalism, a bicameral system, and a separation of legislative from executive power as it is practiced in the United States. I propose that one branch is elected, but can only hold office once in a lifetime, while the other branch consists of average people, getting together to deliberate the merit of a bill upon need. It also requires a federalist system so that local legal initiatives and bills can be discussed locally, at both the municipal and state levels. A citizen might thus be called upon to serve legal duty for his or her city or town, state, or nation. Unicameral political systems and unitarian systems would require a different design.

My proposal is preliminary because practice and experience must inform a community so it can reform and adapt the institutions to govern itself. I believe that the substitution of the House of Representatives with the House of Deliberation is an important first step to democratize democracy everywhere where federalism and bicameras are already a reality—if coupled with term limits and reelection limits of the elected members of the other chamber and other reform outlined above and discussed by such authors as Lawrence Lessig (2019).

Once a House of Deliberation with randomly selected citizens is a reality, party adversary will dramatically decline, thus promising to avoid the kind of gridlock and government shutdown we had to witness over the past years. Corruption, manipulation, interest group influence, the influence of money and corporations, as well as the sort of framing of public issues for the sake of "selling them" to the broader public and the manipulation that goes along with it would most likely all come to an end. The manipulation of elections and the influence of fake news would wither. Average people would rule themselves, as they can and should, in a true democracy.

CHAPTER 3

PREDISTRIBUTION AND UPPER LIMITS

A competition is not fair if not all of us start from the same position. That is the core insight driving this chapter. The other is that competition will never end, if not controlled or limited. At the same time, competition is a powerful engine of innovation and motivation and without it, people tend to not give their best and they do not excel, as we have seen in many real-socialism experiments. The question thus is: how can we preserve the desirable aspects of competition while avoiding its excesses and its abuses?

This chapter elaborates an answer to this question. I argue that competition is desirable and positive—as long as it is fair and kept within acceptable limits. The perverse inequalities in income and wealth we witness today are not fair and they are not justifiable based on effort or work (Alperovitz and Daly, 2008). After all, the average income of an American S&P 500 CEO is around $14.5 million—361 times as much as the income of the average worker in those same companies. No person deserves to earn 361 times more than the other, as it is impossible that someone works 361 times more or carries 361 times the responsibility. The profit made today by simply investing one's money are not based on any tangible effort at all and they are thus not "earned" or "deserved" in any meaningful definition of these terms.

What those "acceptable limits" are will depend and must be decided by those local communities where people have to live and interact with each other. What we do know with certainty is that it is not fair if one person owns half of all the assets of all the villagers or towns people combined—but that is precisely the situation we find ourselves in today, on a global scale.

This chapter will elaborate and explain what new possibilities and perspectives for achieving fairness, equal opportunity, and ecological sustainability open up once we look at this problem from a different angle, through the prism of new paradigms.

SCARCITY AND THE PROBLEM OF RELATIONAL GOODS

In free market societies, we are required to compete fiercely over scarce goods. Scarcity structures the playfield in such a way that everybody has incentives to win over all others, if possible. The logic of scarcity is further reinvigorated by the nature of positional, or relations, goods. These are goods that only deliver their benefits as long as they are not broadly shared. If everybody has a Harvard degree, then the value of such a degree declines dramatically. As more and more people are indeed consuming positional goods, more time and investment are required to achieve the same outcome. Jobs that required a high school diploma in the past new require a master's degree. While the job is the same, the time and investment it now requires to get it has risen dramatically. Scarcity and the nature of positional, or relational, goods are the core reasons for never ending and ever-increasing competition. Under the conditions created by scarcity and positional goods, there is no end in sight for competition. To the contrary, under current conditions, competition will get worse and fiercer. Scarcity and positional competition are thus the core problems any policy seeking to address a sustained and fair future needs to address.

We have created systems where there is not enough for everyone—even if there could be. Under conditions of capitalism and mass society, everyone wants a bigger piece of the pie, but there simply is not enough pie.

If everybody had access to beach houses, the beach will be ruined. If we all had Harvard degrees, those degrees would not be worth much. Therefore, access is restricted and, as a result, we all live in a world with double standards: there is the exquisite service offered to all those who are gold or platinum members—and there is the average service for average people. Next time you fly economy—just take a look into the first-class cabin to get a sense of the truth of this statement. There is only space for so many houses on the beach, so only the rich can afford to live there. The best universities, which lead to the best jobs, are reserved for the rich and the already privileged. Hence, our current solution to this problem of scarcity of resources is one of elitism and exclusive access—and this solution has become highly normalized so that we all tentatively accept it. On moral grounds, however, it is not fair or just to reserve better treatment to the rich.

There are two mechanisms at play that are together responsible for creating this scenario: scarcity and positional competition. Scarcity results from limited goods and unlimited wants whereas positional competition arises from an inherent social dimension of consumption, so that some goods only deliver the desired outcome as long as they are not broadly shared. Both problems are inherent in free market competition—as long as this competition is open-ended and potentially never ending (Hirsch, 1976).

There are a few potential solutions to this double problem. One is to limit wants, which is an approach that is already under way in some of the most advanced capitalist societies, going under the label "degrowth." Degrowth is the voluntary self-limitation of consumption and waste production through the adoption of a more frugal lifestyle. Tim Jackson (2009) has proposed reducing workdays and focusing on quality of life instead of economic growth as the main way to assess our well-being. According to him, implementing measures and policies inspired by this insight would lead to *Prosperity without Growth*, which is the title of his book.

In continental Europe, we can already see people preferring to ride their bike instead of taking a car; spending vacations at home instead of abroad; sharing apartments instead of building their own house, and producing their own vegetables instead of buying them at the supermarket. The tiny-house movement in the United States is another example of this trend. All of these are post-capitalistic strategies that arise once people have experienced that consumption per se does not bring fulfillment or happiness. It is not a strategy that can be demanded from anyone without infringing on their freedom and it is not a strategy that most poor people will readily embrace, given the massive propaganda of consumerism throughout the world. However, as such examples as the Zapatistas in southern Mexico have long demonstrated, "poverty" is but one variable in assessing one's quality of life and there is a growing movement, lead mostly by indigenous and first people of the Americas, to steer clear from consumerism and instead embrace more sustainable lifestyles. After all, poverty is not an emic category of most people and instead a construct created by capitalist economists, unable to capture true quality of life. Degrowth and the embracing of ancestral lifestyles share a denial of blind consumerism as a goal in itself.

The problem of positional consumption is more difficult to tackle, as natural resources are indeed limited. Under free market competition, the solution of market crowding is regulated automatically through higher prices. In such a world, only the rich have access to the "good stuff." This solution is, however, not fair, as long as riches can be passed on to the next generation so that those born rich have access to exclusive goods simply because they were born to the "right" parents.[1]

As Gar Alperovitz and Lew Daly (2008) have shown, those who are rich today have successfully appropriated a social inheritance that rightfully belongs to all. Their inventions, or advances, take advantage of the knowledge, the infrastructure, and the inventions of the past—and they appropriate them for the sake of their own, private benefit. Without the inventions of Newton, Einstein, and Bill Faraday, Bill Gates would have not been able to develop the personal computer. He did not have to start from scratch. The inventions and advancements inherited from Newton, Einstein, and Faraday have made his success possible. To some economists, 80 percent of our current technological advancements are due to this historical dividend—yet its benefits are not spread equally among all of us. In the United States, over 600,000 people apply for patents every year, seeking to secure, for themselves, the benefits of their inventions without given due consideration to the social dividend that allowed them to get there. They take advantage of knowledge, education, and infrastructure available to them and maintained by governments through taxes paid by us all—to secure personal and individual benefits.

The most radical solution to this problem is radical equalization, as proposed and conducted by socialist regimes. The outcome of most of these regimes was and is that we simply have no exclusive things, before only the rich can have them. Given the human condition of strive, this solution is, however, not truly fulfilling, as it impacts our freedom to act negatively. Any solution to the problem of scarcity must take this human strive into account.

The proposal advanced here allows for competition and for winners and losers. It just seeks to institutionalize barriers to limit how great, how often, and for how long one person, one family, and one group can win. Social justice demands that we all have an equal chance to win and lose—and that one individual, one family, or one group cannot win all the time, and another lose all the time, in the different games and competitions we have to enter during our lifetimes (Barry, 2005).

The old paradigms of capitalism and socialism do not contain the tools that help us address this problem. Socialism has lost its creditability and desirability after the world learned what real state socialism meant to all those living under it. Socialism's demise has brought us the triumph of capitalism—but we are now reaching a stage where we need to rethink capitalism for the sake of species survival, justice, and equal opportunity.

In the most advanced capitalist systems on the planet, inequalities and ecological disaster are also the most advanced and fairness and equal opportunity most in jeopardy, due to the riches that some have been able accumulate and the unfair advantages these riches provide them. In the United States, the age-old promise to "make it" through hard work and effort alone is no longer possible.

If you start with nothing, you will simply not be able to compete successfully, let alone win, against the 11 million millionaires and their children currently residing in the United States. To be accepted to a top university and the desirable jobs these universities prepare for, you need money. You can never save enough money to compete against those who start by investing a million dollars. All the nice houses on the beaches of this country and all the nice houses and apartments in California, New York City, and in Miami are already owned—and they cost a fortune. Average people have no systematic chance to win in most competitions against the rich—at least not in those competitions that matter. "Systematic" is a crucial term here. Exceptionally, we will see someone "making it," coming up from the bottom. Fairness demands that we all have a fair chance to win—so that societies are not divided into systematic winners and losers.

To address the problems of equal opportunity, fairness, and also ecological soundness and long-term survival, we need a new economic paradigm.

PREREQUISITES: HIGH QUALITY HEALTH AND EDUCATION

Predistribution means that all people living in a society or country receive equal support to succeed in competitive markets. This would entail offering free quality health care for all. Universal health care is a reality in many countries on the planet, for example, in Canada, the United Kingdom, France, Germany, and Scandinavia. Most Latin American countries offer free, public health care for all—even if there, public providers compete with private ones, which has produced a two-tier system of high quality, "good" private health care and precarious and underfunded "bad" public health.

The Latin American cases teach us a few things: In the Americas, from Canada to Chile, the provision of some sort of universal health care is the norm. In most countries, public health care is simply free, not requiring any insurance. Only the United States does not provide some form of universal health care access to all its citizens in the Western Hemisphere. Most countries of the Americas have mixed public health systems of public and private providers. In most countries, and that is the second lesson, public health systems are precarious and those who can afford it secure themselves privately, thus carrying over economic inequalities into the health sector. Predistribution demands as a prerequisite that average people don't have to worry about their health and that economic wealth does not translate into superior care and, by extension, poverty into substandard care. Free access to high quality health care is a prerequisite for justice and fairness and for predistribution.

High quality education for all is another prerequisite for predistribution. Given that each year of additional formal education significantly adds to lifelog earnings (US males with a college degree earn some $900,000 more during their life compared to those with only a high school diploma) and degrees from Ivy League universities promise about double the income compared to the same degrees earned from other colleges (https://collegescorecard.ed.gov/data/), access to education are central to equal opportunity and fairness.

For the sake of justice and fairness, all schools and universities must offer the same, high quality education and the currently dominant systems of educational stratification must end. This is less outrageous as it may sound to American ears. Most European universities are not ranked and do not compete with each other over prestige and status. In Germany, France, Norway, Finland, and Sweden, all university education is free. In Germany, the right to education includes university education and the right is anchored in Germany's constitution. The American system of extreme educational stratification is indeed an exception and an English legacy. Cambridge and Oxford served as the matrix for the American Ivy Leagues and the creation of educational systems where the best education is afforded to the already privileged and the worst quality education extended to all those who would need it the most is an aristocratic, not a democratic practice.

For the sake of fairness and equal opportunity, this aristocratic Anglo trend must be reversed and high quality education, from kindergarten to university, offered to all entering the education system, but particularly to those entering it with the lowest levels of financial, cultural, and social capital. From a social justice and fairness standpoint, it is the underprivileged that should receive the most educational support, not the already privileged.

Such policies demand, of course, a massive change in policy priorities— away from spending the bulk of public money on war and external affairs to spending it on the well-being and education of a country's own citizenry instead. During most of the 20 years of the US war with Afghanistan, the US government spent more money on the average Afghan citizen through military spending than on the average American. Reversing education and health priorities requires that people, not corporations and the military-industrial complex again take central stage in policies and politics and are made priorities.

Once health and education have been secured for all citizens and taken out of the realm of scarcity, average people will not have to worry any more about how to best secure those basic needs and can direct their energy toward other goals.

EQUAL CHANCES TO WIN

The proposal I am advancing here does not aim at abolishing competition and free markets. Quite the opposite. I argue that if we want to keep competition and free markets around, and we have good reason to do so, then we must regulate them in such a way that competition keeps being fair at every new round and that we avoid the extreme inequalities of today. The traditional approach to achieve this goal is through taxes.

In fact, debates about inheritance and asset limitations are far less radical than they seem at first sight today. The most common policies addressing them are progressive income taxes, taxes on wealth, taxes on inheritances, and taxes on capital transactions (Piketty, 2014). In fact, many countries have progressive income tax regimes, thus charging more taxes to those earning more money. Several countries also tax wealth (France, Spain, Switzerland, Norway, Netherlands, and India), applied in different ways to assets exceeding certain levels, sometimes calling it "solidarity tax" (in France). In addition, most countries have different tax regimes in place for inheritance, gifts, real estate transfers, and endowments. Belgium, the Czech Republic, Denmark, Finland, France, Germany, India, Ireland, Italy, Japan, Luxembourg, the Netherlands, Norway, Philippines, Poland, Portugal, South Africa, South Korea, Spain, Switzerland, Turkey, the UK, and the United States all levy taxes on the transfer of assets from one person to another, upon death or before, using different criteria and allowing for different tax free minimum and maximum asset amounts. (A good source of information on inheritance, asset, and gift taxes is provided by financial planning organizations and investment banks, e.g., by *Ernst&Young*, whose 2013 International Inheritance and Tax guide served me as a source for the above list. It is available online at: http://www.ey.com/Publication/vwLUAssets/2013-international-estate-and-inheritance-tax-guide/$FILE/2013-international-estate-and-inheritance-tax-guide.pdf.)

Different versions of the "Tobin Tax," that is, a tax on financial transactions, initially proposed in the 1990s, continue to surface in today's political debates, advocated by such politicians as Bernie Sanders and like-minded others. The European Commission proposed a financial transaction tax in 2013, but was blocked from imposing it in 2014, 2015, and 2016, mostly by Europe's financial heart: the United Kingdom.

Taxes allow for inequalities to occur and then seek remedying them after the fact. It comes as no surprise that almost everybody is opposed to taxes. Many of those who pay high taxes feel that they are being robbed of the money they have earned. Those who benefit from redistribution schemes, on the other hand, are subjected to state control and surveillance, transforming them into transparent citizens, exposed to often humiliating treatments of bureaucrats. The resulting incentive structure of taxing are negative on both sides: those who pay high taxes have reason to hide their earnings and avoid paying taxes and those benefitting from it have reason to rely on it and avoid work if they can. Counteracting these reasonable and expected behaviors in turn takes much effort, costs a lot of money, and creates a system of institutionalized cheating, surveillance, and punishment. What are the alternatives?

Equal opportunities and fairness demand that we rethink our current educational and health systems in such a way that those most in need receive more service than those already privileged. As the Nobel Prize–winning economist Amartya Sen (2000) has long pointed out, different people have different capabilities to pursue their wants and needs. A fair state system would support those with lower capabilities to live the kind of life they want so they can have an equal, and hence fair, chance to succeed. Similarly, social justice demands that those people with special needs receive more care and support than those who do not have special needs—a notion that is found unproblematic, and fair, by most today.

However, acceptance of this principle of social justice requires a reversal of our current systems, where those already privileged receive better health care and better education compared to the rest of us, thus further bolstering their relative advantages.

Applied to the economic realm in general, this means that fairness and equal opportunity require systems not of redistribution, but of a predistribution in such a way that people with less capabilities and hence less chances to fulfill their wants and needs receive more assistance than those who are already born with more capabilities.

Another way of looking at this is through the lens of capitals: some people are born with high amounts of financial capital. They inherit. Under the current system, high financial capital increases the amounts of other capitals at their disposal: educational, cultural, and social. Their money buys them access.

To be fair, the opposite would have to be enacted: those born with lower amounts of financial capital must receive state support, so they can compete equally. Investment into their educational, health, social, and cultural capitals should also be considered so that the lack of financial capital does not spill over and impact the other capitals. The amount of different capitals a person commands determines their life chances and their ability to be successful, after all.

PREDISTRIBUTION

The only approach, as far as I can conceive, to protect equal opportunity and fairness for all while maintaining competition, free markets, and individual freedom is predistribution, a system where measures are taken to ensure that we all start roughly from the same position *before* we enter competitive systems. This requires the leveling of the playfield with such measures as the payment of reparations to all those who have been pushed to the back of the line and thus not given a fair chance to succeed. I will elaborate the reasoning for reparations later, in a separate chapter.

Predistribution demands that everybody receives government support at the beginning of their economically active lives. Governments would provide start-up funds to citizens in the form of a government donation (Kretzmann and McKnight, 1993; Yunus, 2003; Ackerman and Alstott, 1999). Anthony Atkinson (2015) has called such a policy "Inheritance for All" (Atkinson, 2015: 169), demonstrating that making such a capital endowment available to all citizens when they reach early adulthood would enable all to become active stakeholders and participants in different markets. He suggests financing such a policy with a tax on capital gains. Others have suggested financing it through a tax on personal wealth (Ackerman and Alstott, 1999).

An empirical example to follow is the Alaskan Permanent Fund, which pays annual dividends to Alaskan residents in the amount of some US $2,000 every year. In many countries across the globe, basic citizen income schemes are being debated and enough empirical experiences, including Alaska, already exist to allow for a systematic study of the technical aspects on how to finance such funds.

Social credit systems, as proposed by Clifford Hugh Douglas in the early twentieth century, have been tried in different Canadian provinces and cities. Andrew Yang, a democratic presidential candidate for the 2020 US presidential election, has proposed a US $1,000 basic income, to be financed by a value added tax (VAT) scheme.

While these proposals differ in their application, they all rely on a basic insight, namely that only savings can lead to investments so that all those without any savings are excluded from becoming economically active. By providing them with a stable amount of income, these previously excluded populations could be pushed into economic activity and contribute the overall growth.

Providing young adults with start-up funds in order to increase their capabilities and enlarge their agency seems particularly relevant for those who have been pushed to the back of the line through systematic exclusion and stigmatization. Investing in the economic capabilities of the young in a scenario where excellent education and health care are available to all will prove to be an excellent investment, propelling many into professional careers that would have otherwise not been able to pursue them. Such a policy promises to produce a high return only a few years after the initial investment is made. We can get a glimpse of how successful such a policy is by examining the success of micro finance loans and affirmative action policies. Most of those who benefitted from such policies and are able to attend excellent colleges and universities because of it have become successful professionals and community members (Bok and Bowen, 2000). On average, investment in education has a private return of between 7.4 and 11.7 percent, but an even higher social return, which considers the ability to pay taxes and the money a state saves with decreased incarceration rates and other costs associated with low educational levels (Psacharopoulos, 2012).

It is also worth noting that traditionally, in countries like the United States, Brazil, and South Africa, whites have benefitted from all-white affirmative action policies and other white-only benefits for 200–400 years, thus making them, on average, very successful comparatively. Start-up funds would apply affirmative action to all citizens without family start-up funds in a country. The amounts would need to be determined by need and family legacy, as there are many whose families already provide their children with start-up funds and private affirmative action support by paying for the entrance into highly competitive colleges and universities and by supporting the start-up business of their offspring.

INHERITANCE FOR ALL

What sets today's elites apart from the average citizen is inheritance. Wealth takes generations to accumulate and, given the market dynamics discussed above, many goods can only be obtained by those who secured them early on, before markets got crowded. Wealth, in other words, has a historical dimension. The main mechanism to pass on past privilege to today's generation and thus tilt fairness and equal opportunity toward the rich is inheritance.

To avoid the spillover of parental riches to unfairly supporting the life chances of their children, predistribution policies would have to be combined with absolute restrictions on any personal inheritance. From the perspective of fairness, nobody "deserves" to be born rich—just like nobody deserves to be born poor and destitute. Those born rich do not just inherit money. With it, they inherit opportunities in the form of access to excellent private schools, exclusive college admissions, as well as social and cultural networks and capitals associated with belonging to the "upper crust." None of these inheritances are earned and fair. They all undermine equal opportunity.

If personal inheritance would be eliminated, then funding for start-ups would be secured. Assets left behind after death could then be used to cover the costs of start-up for all in the form of an "inheritance for all" instead of securing undue advantages to the offspring of the rich, as they currently do.

Furthermore, if personal inheritance would be strictly limited or forbidden, then many of the assets that are currently passed on to the next generation, thus serving as building blocks for family dynasties, would reenter common markets and become accessible again to average earners and consumers. Such a policy would invigorate markets tremendously, as it would be the end of the "leisure class"—people who do not work and simply live of their inheritance. Their economic behavior tends to be unproductive, as Thorstein Veblen (2009) has argued many years back. Currently, the assets they own are taken out of common markets, thus diminishing the amount of goods in circulation. The rich are able to shield these assets through exorbitant prices, so that anybody who has to work to earn their money can never afford them. Such a system is neither fair nor economically rational. Furthermore, the existence of such a group of people is not justifiable by merit, hard work, or any of the other core values underpinning democracy. It is simply a matter of "birth luck" and not in accordance with democratic values.

If assets accumulated during a lifetime would return to common markets and become accessible again to all, commonly accessible markets would grow and become invigorated. It would block the construction of intergenerational dynasties and work a great deal to restore fairness and equal opportunity for all. The assets gained by applying such a policy would be able to fund an inheritance for all scheme and allow for start-up funds for all.

Access to first-class education and health care, combined with differential start-up funds for all, financed by the confiscation of all inherited goods, would level the playfield of all to a great extent. It would be a competitive system that is fair, providing all with roughly the same chances to win. It would invigorate markets tremendously, as previously frozen goods would periodically reenter commonly accessible markets. However, such a system would only address fairness and equal opportunity, not scarcity, and only to a very limited extend positional condition. To also address scarcity and positional competition, predistribution needs to be supported by upper limits.

UPPER LIMITS

The only way to protect the planet from devastation and to ensure that resources are preserved is to establish upper limits to income, wealth, and asset holding, which also implies upper limits to economic expansion and growth. At some point very soon, and it appears that we are very close already, we will have reached the carrying capacity of the planet and further growth and economic expansion will no longer be an option. Zero growth strategies and degrowth might at some point in time become required policies to preserve our collective survival. Both of these policies are, however, prone to cause severe reactions and dramatic and partly undesirable change of human sociability. The establishment of upper limits, while there is still time, promises to keep competition alive— within reasonable benchmarks. If combined with high access to quality education, free health care, and predistribution policies, upper limits are a way to control scarcity and positional competition by limiting it. Competition would still exist and there would still be winners and losers, thus keeping free market incentive structures alive—but the winners could not win as obscenely as they currently do. Their winning would also not carry over to the next generation, as long as inheritance is controlled for. Such a policy will lead to a more sustained interaction among humans and between humans and the planet.

Upper limits have the added benefit that they not only are the only conceivable way to protect our collective future on this planet, but they also work toward establishing equal opportunities and fairness. As already mentioned above, it is by no means fair that some of us earn hundreds of times more money than others who also work hard every day. It is simply not fair that the superrich have reserved all the beach houses and nice apartments to themselves. They do not deserve them, if "deserving" is at all related to merit and work, as it should be. Most superrich, in fact, do not work at all. They "let their money work for them"—which is a shallow metaphor for not working. Work, in our current system, has long lost the ability to catch up with the superrich.

Upper limits to wealth and income, coupled with outlawing personal inheritance would also bring down prices of all goods as nobody could sell anything to a price beyond what everybody earns. The scarcity of the housing market in such cities as New York and Los Angeles would be successfully addressed by avoiding the excesses of the superrich.

To rein in the excesses of a system that rewards investment over work, we need to collectively find an answer to the question: what is enough?

Inspiration comes, again, from indigenous groups, some of whom have long established upper limits to how much one person, or one family, can own. As in most indigenous societies, land continues to be the most valuable asset they have, individual and family landownership has limits. What those limits are is defined by the community—as the community also suffers if one person, or family, usurps more land than they can use. While most indigenous communities operate on a smaller scale than most industrial and postindustrial societies, some of the political institutions regulating their political and economic lives are still valuable of consideration as they contain the causal mechanisms for protecting fairness and equal opportunity. Carefully and gradually expanding those institutions tried and tested at a smaller scale is precisely how to ensure success in a larger framework.

Indigenous people, however, are not the only ones who have devised ways to limit the influence of inheritance and upper limits.

UPPER LIMITS AND INHERITANCE AMONG THE AMERICAN FOUNDING FATHERS[2]

The proposal to limit the concentration of wealth is as old as the very idea of democracy. It is also at its core, as I will demonstrate here. To put this into precise language, I argue that addressing inequality by limiting the amount of assets the rich can hold, barring personal inheritance, as well as providing equal opportunities to all by granting the majority equal access to high quality health, and education has always been at the core of democratic thought and is by no means radical or outlandish.

The theme of limiting economic inequality and avoiding that wealth spills over into the political realm has been termed "Greek" or "Athenian" by such authors as Eric Nelson (2004), as it can be traced back to ancient Greek sources. From there, it reemerged almost everywhere where republics were established and where democracy was debated.

Plato writes in his *Laws*:

> Honour is not to be given to the fair body, or to the strong or the swift or the tall, or to the healthy body (although many may think otherwise), any more than to their opposites; but the mean states of all these habits are by far the safest and most moderate; for the one extreme makes the soul braggart and insolent, and the other, illiberal and base; and money, and property, and distinction all go to the same tune. The excess of any of these things is apt to be a source of hatreds and divisions among states and individuals; and the defect of them is commonly a cause of slavery. And, therefore, I would not have any one fond of heaping up riches for the sake of his children, in

order that he may leave them as rich as possible. (Plato 348 BC, translated by Benjamin Jowett, 97f)

For Plato and his world, property and wealth were strongly related to landownership. The concentration of land in but a few hands was perceived as the source of misfortune. Plato offers his solution to this problem in his *Laws*:

How then can we rightly order the distribution of the land? In the first place, the number of the citizens has to be determined, and also the number and size of the divisions into which they will have to be formed; and the land and the houses will then have to be apportioned by us as fairly as we can. (Plato 348 BC, translated by Benjamin Jowett, 105)

According to Nelson (2004), Plato suggests that to ensure happiness to all, "the *polis* must—on grounds of justice—either abolish private property (as in the Republic) or sharply restrict its accumulation (as in the *Laws*)" (Nelson, 2004: 13).

Aristotle agrees with his teacher Plato in his assessment of the corrupting influence of wealth and the need to limit it. According to Fred Miller (1997),

Aristotle's theory of property rights also allows for the regulation of property. Newman remarks that the defence of private property in *Politics*, II 5, is not expressly coupled with qualifications, but Aristotle elsewhere endorses various social policies which limit private property rights. The qualifications upon private property rights should probably be understood in the light of the fact that they are, for Aristotle, subordinate to political rights. His defence of private property is not intended as a case for total privatization. Presumably on similar grounds, he advocates coercive taxation for the purposes of defence and internal needs (VII 8 1328^b10-11; III 12 1283^a17-18). He also recommends support for needy citizens, as virtuous acts carrying out his policy of "private ownership, common use" (VII 10 $1329^b41-1330^a2$; VI 6 1320^b2-11). The provisos which he attaches to natural acquisition can explain his advocacy of legal limits on the amount of land any citizen can own (see VI 4 1319^a8-10). He also recommends that individuals do not have the liberty to sell and bequeath land however they please (II 9 1270^a18-21). He even admits that the ostracism of very rich or powerful citizens may be justified by a sort of political justice (see III 13 1284^b15-34; VI 8 1308^b19). The point here is probably that the excessive exercise of property and other rights by some persons jeopardizes the political rights of the other citizens, and that the political rights of the latter should override the property rights of the former. (Miller, 1997: 329–30)

In his *Constitution of Athens*, Aristotle quotes Solon, called upon by the Athenians after civil war had broken out between the rich landholders and the common people. Solon, a poet and himself a commoner, lived from 638 to about 558 BCE, thus a good century before Plato (428–348 BCE) and Aristotle (384–322 BC) and has this to say on the issue of limiting the assets of the wealthy and their influence on politics:

> But ye who have store of good, who are sated and overflow, Restrain your swelling soul, and still it and keep it low: Let the heart that is great within you be trained a lowlier way; Ye shall not have all at your will, and we will not for ever obey. (Aristotle, Book one, Part 5, translated by Sir Frederic G. Kenyon)

And Aristotle continues:

> Indeed, he constantly fastens the blame of the conflict on the rich; and accordingly at the beginning of the poem he says that he fears "the love of wealth and an overweening mind," evidently meaning that it was through these that the quarrel arose. (Aristotle, Book one, Part 5, translated by Sir Frederic G. Kenyon)

To end the war of the nobles against the commoners and, in Aristotle's words, "the oppression of the many by the few," Solon ended slavery among citizens, cancelled debts, and created the council of 400. The Athenians thus were decisively opposed to the concentration of wealth in few hands and favored policies that either protected equal access to land or, once lost, restored it. Most treaties focus on land, as it must be thought of as the main asset a man, or a family, could hold, thus bequeathing unequal opportunities to the head of the family and his offspring.

While the Romans living under the republic differed in their approach to justice and liberty from the Athenians, they nevertheless shared their concern for the evils growing out of excessive wealth and power. Here, as in Athens, wealth was strongly associated with landownership and the dispute over land is one that characterizes the entire duration of the republic, culminating in the reforms proposed by the Gracchi brothers.

Tiberius Gracchus was elected tribune in 133 BCE and proposed a law making it illegal for any person to possess more than 500 *iugera* (about 300 acres or 121 hectares) of public land and for any family to own more than 1,000 *iugera*. He was killed in that same year by opposing senators and their supporters. His brother, Gaius, subsequently served two consecutive terms as tribune, which he used to advance an agenda very similar to his brother's. He, too, was killed, together with 3,000 supporters, without trial (Le Glay, 2009). The violence and the extra-legal ways in which the Gracchi brothers were dealt with by powerful Roman senators, and their followers, point at the level of contestation the question of limited landownership faced. While for the Gracchi, land reform was essential and a sine qua non condition to protect Rome from civil war and rural decay—powerful senators and latifundio owners, while they might have agreed with the diagnosis, acted in the defense of their own privileges. Throughout the republic, Roman ordinary citizens made several attempts at limiting the power of the aristocratic senators, at times formally, through their tributes, at times through protest and violence.

Eric Nelson (2004) provides a detailed analysis on how Greek thought on equality and justice has influenced republican thought in general and the American republican tradition in particular. From his detailed account it becomes clear that not only the Founding Fathers, but also a whole array of American public leaders active around the time of American independence, had subscribed to the ideas of Plato and Aristotle—as well as those of Machiavelli and James Harrington. Many of the proposals advanced during the late eighteenth and early nineteenth centuries favored imposing limits to wealth accumulation, limits to intergenerational wealth transfer, and institutions, as well as laws, able to fend off the undue influence of the rich onto politics and public affairs in general. This topic was also discussed in the Federalist Papers (particularly Federalist 10) and preached by different, republican-minded clerics in the young American republic.

In fact, when the Pennsylvania Declaration of Rights was discussed by the Philadelphia Congress in July and August 1776, it originally contained an article (No. 16), which I already quoted above. It stated, "That an enormous Proportion of Property vested in a few individuals is dangerous to the Rights, and destructive of the Common Happiness, of Mankind; and therefore every free State hath the Right by its Laws to discourage the Possession of such Property."[3]

Article 16 of the Pennsylvania Declaration of Rights, which acted under the leadership of Benjamin Franklin, was later deleted and substituted with another, quite different article, which contained no more references to large and excessive property. However, the fact that it was part of the Declaration at one point highlights the importance and the centrality of this concern among the American Founders. Thomas Jefferson was particularly outspoken about the undue influence of wealth on politics. He took inspiration not just from Plato, Aristotle, and Montesquieu, but also from James Harrington (1611–77), who himself based his claims on Plato, Aristotle, and Machiavelli and argues:

> For equality of estates causes equality of power, and equality of power is the liberty, not only of the commonwealth, but of every man. (Harrington, 2006: 8)

The solution, for Harrington, to existing inequalities in wealth and power is to limit access to them. In his utopian *Oceana*, he ordains:

> That every man who is at present possessed, or shall hereafter be possessed, of an estate in land exceeding the revenue of £2,000 a year, and having more than one son, shall leave his lands either equally divided among them, in case the lands amount to above £2,000 a year to each, or no near equally, in case they come under, that the greater part or portion of the same remaining to the eldest exceed not the value of £2,000 revenue. And no man, not in present possession of lands above the value of £2,000 by the year, shall receive, enjoy (except by lawful inheritance) acquire, or, purchase to himself lands within the said territories, amounting, with those already in his possession, above the said revenue. (Harrington, 1656: 60)

Harrington also defends universal access to education, which, he argues, should be free of charge to the poor. Harrington greatly influenced Thomas Jefferson, who in his autobiography favored an inheritance law able to break up family fortunes and thus avoid the emergence of a money aristocracy. In a letter to John Adams, Jefferson writes:

> At the first session of our legislator after the Declaration of Independence, we passed a law abolishing entails. And this was followed by one abolishing the privilege of Primogeniture, and dividing the lands of intestates equally among all their children, or their representatives. These laws, drawn by myself, laid the axe to the root of Pseudo-aristocracy. And had another which I prepared been adopted by the legislature, our work would have been compleat. It was a Bill for the more general diffusion of learning [...] Worth and genius would thus have been sought out from every condition

of life, and compleatly prepared by education for defeating the competition of wealth and birth for public trust. (The Adams-Jefferson Letter, p. 390, quoted in Nelson, 2004: 203)

To James Madison, Jefferson writes:

I am conscious that an equal division of property is impractical, but the consequences of this enormous inequality producing so much misery to the bulk of mankind, legislators cannot invent too many devices for subdividing property, only taking care to let their subdivisions go hand in hand with the natural affections of the human mind. (Jefferson, Writings, p. 841, quoted in Nelson, 2004: 204f)

John Locke is equally supportive of imposing limits to ownership of land, stating, in his *Second Treatise on Government*, that in the state of nature, men did not hold more land than they could use.

James Madison agrees and argues:

The great object should be to combat evil: 1. By establishing political equality among all. 2. By withholding unnecessary opportunities from the few, to increase the inequality of property, by an immoderate, and especially an unmerited, accumulation of wealth. 3. By silent operation of laws, which, without violating the rights of property, reduce extreme wealth to a state of mediocrity, and raise extreme indigence towards a state of comfort. (*The Papers of James Madison*, vol. XIV, 1983: 197, quoted in Nelson, 2004: 207)

Adam Smith approaches the same subject—even if not so much from a moral standpoint, but in terms of economic efficiency and market distortions resulting from monopoly pricing—the unavoidable result, he thought, of hoarding great amounts of land in but a few hands. Smith argues that primogeniture affects markets negatively in that it withholds land from markets, concentrating it into the unproductive hands of the few. He states:

The small quantity of land [...] which is brought to the market, and the high price of what is thither, prevents a great number of capitals from being employed in its cultivation and improvement which would otherwise have taken that direction. (Smith, 1976: 384)

Smith further argues that "if landed estates [...] were divided equally among all the children, upon the death of any proprietor who left a numerous family, the estate would generally be sold. So much land would come to market, that it could no longer sell at a monopoly price" (Smith, 1976: 423).

John Adams is equally supportive of making land accessible to all by limiting the amount of land one person can hold. He writes:

> The only possible way, then, of preserving the balance of power on the side of equal liberty and public virtue, is to make the acquisition of land easy to every member of society; to make a division of land into small quantities, so that the multitude may be possessed of landed estates. (Adams, Works, vol. IX, p. 376, quoted in Nelson, 2004: 209)

Arguments about imposing limits on property and asset holding were, at least during the early days of the American Republic, rather commonplace—even if they were controversial and perceived as such. To many of the participating debaters, be it Jefferson, Madison, or the young John Adams, imposing limits on the ownership of land seemed inevitable if the protection of virtue and justice were the goal. The way to achieve a broader spread of property was to abolish entail and primogeniture inheritance—which was achieved by Jefferson. As he explains, this strategy relied on the then-common reality of families counting on a large group of offspring, among which the land could be divided. It also focused on the main asset available for the accumulation of wealth: landownership. To Henry George, the American worker turned thinker and philosopher and author of *Progress and Poverty* (first published in 1879), it was clear that asset concentration undermined equal opportunity for all and created poverty. He argues, "Poverty deepens as wealth increases; wages fall while productivity grows" (George, 2006: 180). George understood that this was caused by the undue accumulation of assets, which provided undue privileges and rents, undermining the opportunities of all those who could not count on such wealth privileges. The only solution, to George, who during his lifetime was the third most famous person in the United States (after Mark Twain and Thomas Edison, according to Agnes George de Mille, his daughter), was to make land common property. According to his daughter,

> Georgists believe in private enterprise, and in its virtues and incentives to produce at maximum efficiency. It is the insidious linking together of special privilege, the unjust outright private ownership of natural or public

resources, monopolies, franchises, that produce unfair domination and autocracy. The means of producing wealth differ at the root: some is thieved from the people and some is honestly earned. George differentiated; Marx did not. The consequences of our failure to discern lie at the heart of our trouble. (Agnes George de Mille, in George, 2006: 308)

Thus, Henry George, similar to the American Founding Fathers, recognized the long-term distortions growing out of asset concentration and monopoly capital. Undue privilege and rent seeking, to him, lay at the heart of poverty amid progress and richness. Similar to the Founding Fathers, his focus was on land.

Transferred to our days, with reduced family sizes and asset holding no longer grounded in land, the set of policies proposed then translate today into the need for general limitations on asset holdings and the splitting up of property and assets in general after the death of a family head—be it for the sake of protection justice, democracy, and general happiness (Jefferson) or to protect markets from monopoly pricing on assets artificially made scarce through hoarding (Smith). All involved debaters were also well aware of the kind of opportunity hoarding that results from entering competitive markets already endowed with assets and of the negative effects the rich exercise on politics.

This theme did not die with the American Founding Fathers. It was picked up in Europe by communists and anarchists around the time of Karl Marx and Mikhail Bakunin and the First Communist International, in 1919. Anarchists, in particular, spoke out for strong inheritance taxes as a way to limit the passing on of privilege from one generation to the next. Such iconic figures as Pierre-Joseph Proudhon, Mikhail Bakunin, and Peter Kropotkin made history when they opposed the state and party-led proposals of the communists. The utopian socialists also contributed significantly to this history of the idea of asset limitation. Charles Fourier, Robert Owen, and the followers of Leo Tolstoy all sought to create societies without hierarchies and without rule over others. The French Communards were able to put these principles into practice—if only for some two months, in 1871. In Germany of 1918, soldiers and citizens established councils inspired by anarchism and libertarian socialism—defending the idea that private property needs to be limited (or abolished) for the sake of general happiness. Anarchism gained another chance in 1936, when the Spanish civil war dealt a blow to the monarchy and opened the door for the formation of local councils and associations. All the while, in great parts of Africa and Latin America, indigenous groups practiced communal landownership, land rotations among community members, and collective land holding. In Europe, commons and other forms of collective land- or forest ownership were present in rural communities and continue to exist to this day (Ostrom, 2015).

On December 15, 1868, the International Alliance of Socialist Democracy was founded by Mikhail Bakunin and given a program. This program states:

1. The Alliance declares itself atheist; it wants abolition of cults, substitution of science for faith and human justice for divine justice.
2. It wants above all political, economic, and social equalization of classes and individuals of both sexes, *commencing with abolition of the right of inheritance* (my emphasis), so that in future enjoyment be equal to each person's production, and so that, in conformity with the decision taken at the last workers' congress in Brussels, the land, instruments of labor, like all other capital, on becoming collective property of the entire society, shall be used only by the workers, that is, by agricultural and individual associations.
3. It wants for all children of both sexes, from birth, equal conditions of development, that is, maintenance, education, and training at all degrees of science, industry, and the arts, being convinced that this equality, at first only economic and social, will increasingly lead to a great natural equality of individuals, eliminating all kinds of artificial inequalities, historical products of a social organization as false as it is iniquitous.
4. Being the foe of all despotism, not recognizing any political form other than republican and rejecting completely any reactionary alliance, it also rejects any political action which does not have as its immediate and direct aim the triumph of the workers' cause against capital.[4]

Communists, anarchists, and libertarian socialists, while differing greatly in their analysis and approach, all saw the accumulation of wealth in a few hands as harmful to the general happiness, to widespread economic prosperity, and to self-rule. Similarly, the provision of free public education was perceived by all as a prerequisite for freedom.

While communism and anarchism were quickly bedeviled and labeled "radical" and antithetic to democracy, the American Founding Fathers, as I hope to have demonstrated, were equally committed to the same goals of avoiding the concentration of wealth and power in a few hands. They were also equally committed to passing laws that actively worked against this concentration of wealth and political power—and for the broader distribution of these assets and the opportunities they provided. It is thus too easy and wrong to dismiss these proposals as "communist."

PROPERTY-OWNING DEMOCRACY

Contemporary mainstream economists and philosophers continue to debate new and innovative ways on how to protect equal opportunity, fairness, and political equality.

James Edward Meade, a British economist (1907–95), received the Nobel Memorial Prize in economic sciences in 1977—after having published *Efficiency, Equality, and the Ownership of Property* in 1965. In this book, Meade introduces the concept of "property-owning democracy." Meade explains:

> Arrangements which encourage the accumulation of property by those with little property are certainly as important as those which discourage further accumulation or encourage dispersal of their fortunes by large property owners [...] the extreme importance of education as a form of investment which affects earning power. (Meade, 1965: 59)

Meade was hardly a radical. He served as a lecturer and later professor at Oxford, the London School of Economics, and Cambridge University and his proposals resonate strongly with those proposed by the ancient Greeks, the American Founding Fathers, and many libertarian socialists and anarchists.

Meade's proposal of a property-owning democracy also did not die with him. John Rawls (2001) integrated his approach into his own *Theory of Justice*. Rawls, to be sure, focuses his attention on the institutional requirements able to protect justice and fairness. In his book *Justice as Fairness: A Restatement* (2001), Rawls aims "to sketch in more detail the kind of background institutions that seem necessary when we take seriously the idea that society is a fair system of cooperation between free and equal citizens from one generation to the next" (Rawls, 2001: 136).

Rawls finds only two systems that are able to create the necessary background conditions for ensuring his two principles of justice: fairness and equal opportunity. These are liberal socialism and property-owning democracy. He rules out laissez-faire capitalism, welfare state capitalism, and state socialism. When comparing those two, he concludes that only property-owning democracy is able to secure fairness and equal opportunity. It is worth quoting him at length:

> The background institutions of property-owning democracy work to disperse the ownership of wealth and capital, and thus to prevent a small part of society from controlling the economy, and indirectly, political life as well. By contrast, welfare-state capitalism permits a small class to have a near monopoly of the means of production. Property-owning democracy

avoids this, not by redistribution of income to those with less at the end of each period, so to speak, but rather by ensuring the widespread ownership of productive assets and human capital (that is, education and trained skills) at the beginning of each period, all this against the background of fair equality and opportunity. The intent is not to simply assist those who lose out through accident or misfortune (although that must be done), but rather to put all citizens in a position to manage their own affairs on a footing of a suitable degree of social and economic equality. (Rawls, 2001: 139)

While John Rawls is notoriously vague about the concrete steps a society must take to institute justice, fairness, and equal opportunities, Amartya Sen (2009) points at capabilities and freedom as the ultimate goals where societal and individual development must meet. With this, Sen opens the door for thinking about the specific needs and opportunities concrete individuals and groups encounter, and require, to fulfill their wishes and needs. Similar to Rawls, the only system that can provide equal and fair opportunities for all, in every generation, is one where investments in education and assets are distributed equally *before* individuals and groups enter into competitive situations. As Martin O'Neill and Thad Williamson (2014) have recently demonstrated, the proposals of both Rawls and Sen point to a system of "predistribution" rather than one of post-factum redistribution. Accordingly, Sen writes, in his *The Idea of Justice* (2009):

Equality was not only among the foremost revolutionary demands in eighteenth-century Europe and America, there has also been an extraordinary consensus on its importance in the Post-Enlightenment world [...]. Equality is demanded in some basic form even by those who are typically seen as having disputed the "case for equality" and expressed skepticism about the central importance of "distributive justice." For example, Robert Nozick may not lean towards equality of utility (as James Meade does), or towards equality of holding of primary goods (as John Rawls does), and yet Nozick does demand equality of libertarian rights—that no one person should have any more right to liberty than anyone else. (Sen, 2009: 291)

In this, the liberal proposals advanced by Rawls and Sen meet the socialist approach advanced by Marxist economists Samuel Bowles and Herbert Gintis (1998), who argue that smart asset distribution can achieve the twin goals of enhancing economic efficiency and equality. This is, in turn, where Marxist scholarship meets the Yale economist Jacob Stewart Hacker (2011), who coined the term "predistribution." He argues:

To protect and restore the hallmarks of a well-functioning market democracy, progressives in the United States and elsewhere must rebuild its institutional foundations and shift back the uneven organisational balance between concentrated economic interests and the broad public. (Hacker, 2011: 1)

Hacker is a member of the British Policy Network, which has close ties to the British Labour Party. In an even more recent treatment, Sir Anthony Atkinson (2015), the British economist, has argued for a lifetime capital receipts tax, which would work against, to some degree, the ability to pass on accumulated wealth to the next generation.

The theme of protecting equal opportunities in markets and politics thus has a long pedigree, reaching back to ancient Athens. It resurfaces among republicans of all sorts—from anarchists to liberals and conservatives. All of them have given asset limitations some thought as all of them have understood that to protect equal opportunity and fairness in competitive markets, all participants must enter those markets equipped with the same assets and capitals. Universal education, and sometimes universally provided health care, also play central roles in the thinking of all those concerned with equal opportunity and fairness. Those who have pressed these questions the furthest all seem to agree that the inheritance of unearned assets provides those who benefit from them with unfair advantages—ultimately not justifiable in a democracy. They all agree that for the sake of equal opportunity, it is not enough to first let inequality and unfairness play out—only to address them later through some sort of redistribution. At that late moment, the damages inequality cause are already done and it is too late to address them while also creating undue the moral hazards. Instead, the central concern of all the authors discussed above is how to predistribute in order to level the playfield—before people enter the public realm, which necessarily contains competitive markets.

What all of these attempts have in common is that they seek to protect equal opportunity and fairness over generations by curbing the influence and power of multinational corporations and the rich. The case for asset distribution and limitation is core to the democratic ideal.

HOW MUCH IS ENOUGH—AND WHO DECIDES?

Upper limits are the counterpart to predistribution. They operate on the other end of the spectrum. Predistributions and reparations support those who have been pushed to the back of the line so they can move up and start the race from a similar position. Upper limits ensure that competitions do not get out of hand while zero-inheritance makes sure that advantages do not spill over into the next race and the next generation. These policies also ensure that the few do not eat half the pie—leaving the majority to fight over the other half. Overconsumption, after all, is not only hurtful to the planet, but it also diminishes the amount of goods in circulation on average markets. Again, think of a village where one family owns half of all the land and half of all the houses. At this point, our planet is such a village.

As current inequalities are deeply entrenched, they need to be addressed on both ends—by supporting those who tend to systematically loose out and by curtailing those who have been winning for generations.

Upper limits to income and wealth are our only chance, the way I see it, to preserve competitive systems and avoid totalitarian solutions while also preserving the biodiversity of this planet and our collective future.

The most challenging problem of establishing upper limits to income and wealth is the decision about what these upper limits should be—and who should determine them. There are no easy solutions for this problem. On one side, it seems obvious that if 1 percent of the world's population owns 50 percent of all assets, then we would collectively all be better off if we distributed the assets of the top 1 percent. In 2019, there were some 2,200 billionaires worldwide, controlling a combined net worth of some US $9 trillion. Clearly, anything over US $1 million in net worth is too much, particularly when considering that the average wealth per adult worldwide is about $63,000.

However, answers to these complicated questions would not have to be found in absolute terms and also not on a world scale. In accordance with the overall theme of this book, decisions about how much is too much must be made democratically, by those local communities where rich members live. It should be informed by criteria of justice and fairness so that abuse by the few is avoided.

Upper limits to wealth and asset holding could be applied to how many houses a single person can own, or how many cars, and how much land. Bolivia has constitutionally restricted landownership to 5,000 hectares, which is still very large and certainly too large for countries where average farm sizes are under 60 hectares, like it is in Germany. In general, the debate about upper limits should start from average values and engage in a public debate about the percentage, or degrees to which one person or one family can surpass the average. If the average farm size in Germany is 60 hectares, then a debate, best conducted by randomly selected farmers from among the different regions of the country, should deliberate and decide to what percentage a single person or family can surpass the average. This number ought to be high enough to encourage people to work hard to succeed, thus maintaining the incentive structures of capitalist systems, yet low enough to avoid the most grotesque distortions we currently witness.

On a basic level, the answer to the question *how much is enough* must be related to work and effort. One person can certainly work twice, maybe three times as hard as another. Some people carry many responsibilities. Maybe a CEO carries five times the responsibilities of the average worker in the same company and maybe—maybe—he or she works twice as hard (which is very doubtful). However, currently the average salary of a CEO in a S&P 500 US company is 361 times the salary of the average worker. It is simply impossible to work 361 times as much as another person or carry 361 times as much responsibility.

Upper limits, in my assessment, should not reach beyond 10 times the average. The median household income in the United States was about $60,000 in 2020. If a 10 times as much upper limit would find acceptance in public debate, then $600,000 would be the upper limit for annual household earnings in the United States.

The debate about upper limits to income must involve all sectors of society, randomly selected, and deliberated at the House of Deliberations.

Provisions could be made within companies, limiting the ratio of earning differentials between CEOs and average workers and in communities and cities with regard to how many houses and how much property one person or family can own. To avoid that some people circumvent such limits by owning different assets in different places, national upper limits for wealth and income would need to be established.

As stock ownership is the main platform where inequalities play out today, such debates would need to include upper limits to how many securities a person, or family, can hold and certain financial instruments and organizations, like hedge funds, should be assessed for their necessity and contribution to our collective well-being. I suspect that many of them will be found to not contribute at all to our collective well-being and even less to our common future and I am fairly certain that outlawing those will bring us nothing but benefits.

CONCLUSION

Predistribution and upper limits to income and wealth, combined with a strict enforcement of zero inheritance promise to achieve equal opportunity, fairness, and hence justice on competitive markets—every new generation. These policies also promise to reintroduce frozen assets into general accessible markets, accessible by average earners and consumers. As such, these policies promise to at once invigorate markets and limit them at the same time. Market mechanisms would be protected, but their impact on live chances limited. Goods would be reintroduced into general markets after they have been accumulated by one person in what would essentially be a "recycle economy."

At the same time, upper limits would put a limit to economic expansion and stop excessive and ever-expanding production and consumption from undermining the very subtract of our survival, our shared ecosystem. Endless growth is responsible for the ecological disaster we already face, and no amount of smart technology can change this threat. Short of zero growth and degrowth, upper limits promise to put an upper limit to economic expansion. If applied to a worldwide scale, as it should, it would also help to establish a fairer worldwide system and work against the current reality where some, rich, countries destroy the planet for all of humanity, as here, again, the poor of this world carry no blame but suffer most of the results of the irresponsible behavior of the rich minority.

It is imperative that we enter into a recycle economy where goods and assets are reintroduced into our systems after their usage as there simply is not enough planet for the excessive and expansive consumption of 8 billion people, let alone of the 10 billion we are projected to reach in 30 years.

CHAPTER 4

REPARATIONS[1]

This chapter is dedicated to a special form of differentiated preredistribution aimed at achieving justice and equal opportunities: reparations for those whose ancestors have been enslaved and used to construct the riches of their enslavers. The basic insight driving this chapter is that wealth constructed in the past casts a long shadow into the future—and so does the lack of wealth. Up to this point, this book has not discussed the racial dimension of poverty and wealth, where "race" is understood here not as a biological reality but as the result of "race-making" or "racialization." Racialization is the social process of systematically discriminating a group of people and thus forcing them to find a commonality among themselves. This commonality is one of experiencing shared discrimination, mistreatment, and disdain by the hands of the majority. "Races" are thus forged, not born and most of those who today perceive themselves as a race did not perceive themselves as such before they became victims of systematic and enduring discrimination.

Given the insight, discussed above, that today's well-being and the chances to succeed and at times win in the different competitive systems that make up our daily lives, I would be remiss not to include a chapter on one of the most pernicious and cruel ways of how one group of people was forcefully pushed to the back of the line and not allowed to compete at all, the enslaved. Slavery affected many groups of people. In the Americas, the first to suffer from it were indigenous people. After most indigenous people of the Americas were extinct, Africans became the next group to help slaveholding whites accumulate the riches that they bring to bear in order to protect the success of their offspring to this day. In this chapter, I will focus on the United States and on African Americans. However, very similar chapters could be written about Native American people of all the Americas and the Caribbean as well as about Africans brought to other parts of colonial America. The United States, after all, only absorbed some 400,000 enslaved Africans. Brazil received at least ten times more and the

Caribbean became the forced exile of some 2 million Africans kidnaped from their homes, families, and motherlands.

Finally, it is important to note that while slavery was the beginning of the systematic mistreatment and the discrimination of Native American, indigenous, First People, as well as enslaved Africans, it was not the end of their unfair treatment. By all accounts, slavery lasted until the 1950s in the United States under the guise of forced labor and false imprisonments in the American South and systematic discrimination on the educational, health, and housing markets lasted at least until the late 1960s here (Blackmon, 2009). In some South and Central American countries, as well as in some parts of the Caribbean where no civil rights movement pressed for an end of discrimination, unfair practices continue to this day, even if they are not recognized and not part of the official laws, as they were in the United States.

African Americans were disproportionally affected by the initial exclusion of farm and domestic workers from the New Deal and the social security protections it brought to white workers during the Great Depression. Even after the 1950s, as Ta-Nehisi Coates (2014) and Michelle Alexander (2020) have shown, discriminatory practices and policies continued to hamper the prospects of African Americans. They were, and continue to be, in some counties and states, the victims of discriminatory housing policies and practices, barring them from partaking in the number one avenue of American middle-class wealth accumulation: real estate ownership. While 73 percent of white American families are home owners, only 41 percent of black Americans fell into this category in 2019 (https://www.statista.com/statistics/500069/homeownership-rates-usa-by-ethnicity/).

Homeownership translates into wealth. According to US Federal Reserve data, in 2016, white families had a median net worth of $171,000 compared to $17,600 for blacks (Dettling, et al., 2017). Homeownership and redlining also drastically impact educational prospects, as poor school districts, under the current system, count on poor schools, offering poor education. Poor education for the already poor and disadvantaged, in turn, disadvantages them further and stifles their prospects for a bright future—particularly if they have to complete against those whose wealth and privilege provides them with excellent opportunities. Reparations, that is, targeted support for those whose ancestors have not been able to provide them with any sort of start-up capital—financial, social, cultural, and otherwise, are thus a requirement of justice and equal opportunity today.

In this chapter, I will also draw some lessons from the way Germany has faced up to its past of enslavement and genocide in order to highlight an important component of reparations, the punishment and expropriation of those riches accumulated through slave labor. Justice, again, demands not only that all people have equal opportunities and that those who have suffered in the past are targeted with special policies aimed at increasing their capabilities; it also demands that those who have unduly enriched themselves by exploiting others and who then passed on these riches to their descendants, providing them with unfair advantages, are held accountable. Paralleling the logic already outlined above, it is not the formerly enslaved and their descendants who brought us this situation of unjustifiable inequality and indeed abhorrent moral disaster; it is those who captured, enslaved, mistreated, discriminated, and abused others in order to advance their own interests whom we need to consider first and foremost when seeking to remedy and address the ills of racism, past and present.

JUSTICE

Justice cannot be achieved today as long as the injustices of the past have not been addressed and counteracted. This is so on moral grounds, and also because past advantages carved out by one group in detriment to another tend to be reproduced to protect and defend the privileges achieved by the dominant group. Under open market conditions in capitalist systems, there is no catching up with those who entered competitive markets earlier and with more assets. The American economist Fred Hirsch already argued in 1976: "What the wealthy have today can no longer be delivered to the rest of us tomorrow" (Hirsch, 1976: 67).

Applied to the situation of the contemporary United States and other countries that practiced systematic slavery over extended periods of time, this also means that black America as a group can never catch up with white America anywhere in the former slaveholding Americas under conditions of free market competition. There simply is no catching up to a group that benefits today from a history of centuries of all-white exclusive access: in the United States, black individuals were forcefully denied legal personhood until 1866, barred from the plain exercise of their political and economic rights until 1964, and they are discriminated against in such crucial areas as homeownership to this very day. In some parts of the United States, unlawful imprisonment and forced labor continued to perpetuate actual slavery until the 1950s (Blackmon, 2009), providing undue advantages to white Americans to the detriment of black Americans. Given the multiplying effect of homeownership on wealth and education, African Americans are facing disadvantages today that are rooted in the past. Considering the devastating psychological effects of systematic dehumanization and racism practiced against a people, African Americans are disadvantaged, their culture deemed unworthy, their aesthetics "ugly," their abilities disregarded and distorted.

White America constructed a system during slavery that allowed white Americans to succeed while blocking the success of black Americans. As a result, current "color-blind" policies increase past disadvantages separating white from black America. While I focus on black versus white America in this chapter, very similar mechanisms are at work when contrasting indigenous, or native America from white America.

Justice should be our guiding principle when debating recognition and reparations. The promise of recognition and reparations is precisely to move beyond racialization to a point where differences in appearance and culture become non-consequential and interchangeable, so that different groups can form at different times, responding to different exogenous incentives.

We are far away from such a scenario today, everywhere. Instead, in all postcolonial societies, coloniality is still a reality, pushing the formerly colonized and enslaved into one group and allowing the former colonizers and slavers into another. One is still systematically on top while the other, composed in reality of a variety of subgroups, is still systematically on the bottom of almost all categories we can think of: wealth, income, education, incarceration rates— even life expectancy itself.

This is so, I argue in this chapter, precisely because history casts a long shadow into the present and the future. Justice requires that we all start from roughly the same positions, but colonialism and slavery have allowed some to start securing their leading positions some one hundred to almost four hundred years *before* others were allowed to even start competing.

Only when past wrongdoing is addressed, recognized, and rectified can we hope to move on into a better, more just, and fair future and only after that can we hope to lift the shame and the guilt from the shoulders of white America so it can start interacting with black and indigenous America in a normal way, unburdened from the weight of the past.

Skeptics might argue that this is not only impractical but also impossible to achieve. It might as well be. But we have to try—if justice is our aim. And justice must be the foundation for our common future, or else we risk splitting further apart into different communities who resent each other for their unjust, inherited privileges, or their "depravity."

DEEP DIVISION

While the scope of this chapter includes all formerly slaveholding societies, most data is available on the United States and I thus propose to generalize from the information available in this country. In the United States, the consequences of a past of slavery, exploitation, exclusion from legal personhood, exclusion from political rights, and denial of civil rights are all too obvious today. Some 20 percent of African Americans today are poor—compared to 10 percent of whites and Asians. Wealth, already mentioned above, is even more distorted, with white families controlling about 10 times as much wealth as black families, on average.

The situation of white privilege vis-à-vis black poverty and exclusion is not much different in any of those American countries that relied on slave labor. In most of them, white elite pacts were forged with the intent to hold former slaves and their descendants out of the benefits of citizenship. Such pacts have been described for Brazil, Colombia, Peru, Jamaica, Haiti and the French Caribbean, Cuba, and Mexico. The comprehensive work on race and colorism in Latin America produced by Edward Telles (2014) shows that discrimination directed against those with darker skin colors has been an integral element in the construction of social hierarchies everywhere in the Americas—from Canada to Tierra del Fuego.

The contemporary situation of all the Americas cannot be adequately explained without taking the past of chattel slavery into account, as it was during the time of slavery and its immediate aftermath that a racial stigma was created and associated with brown skin color. Put simply, the descendants of formerly enslaved Africans today still suffer from the stigmatization that was imposed on their ancestors' bodies centuries ago. Consequently, blacks as a group are likely to be perceived by whites as potentially problematic, underachieving, prone to criminal activity, and so on. Racial stigmatization affects the group as a whole and it is a cognitive process linked to slavery and "rational" in the narrow sense economists apply this term. The end result is that Africans and their descendant are not perceived as partaking in the same humanity as non-blacks (Loury, 2002).

Beyond the cognitive bias, white supremacy constitutes a political system of rule that elevates whites and disparages blacks in systematic ways, as "whiteness has a cash value" (Lipsitz, 1998: vii). In detailed accounts covering laws, immigration, military politics, emotions and desires, identity politics, and consumer patterns, sociologist George Lipsitz demonstrates how most US whites, unless they develop an actively anti-racist identity, reproduce white identity politics because they benefit from it daily and concretely.

Carol Anderson (2017), in turn, has shown that white America has reacted systematically with resentment against black progress every time it occurs, calling the response "white rage." Invoking the work of Charles Mills (1997) on the "racial contract" as well as the research of Richard Rothstein (2017), Anderson argues:

> White rage is not about visible violence, but rather it works its way through the courts, the legislature, and a range of government bureaucracies. It wreaks havoc subtly; almost imperceptibly [...]. The trigger for white rage, inevitably, is black advancement. It is not the mere presence of black people that is the problem; rather, it is blackness with ambition, with drive, with purpose, with aspiration, and with demands for full equal citizenship. (2017: xv)

These arguments provide the basis upon which Juliet Hooker (2009) argues that in today's United States, solidarity among the citizenry is still divided along the color line: the stigmatization of black Americans is so pervasive that most non-blacks simply do not perceive them as an integral part of their political community. Once the political, cognitive, and normative grounds of racial injustice in the United States and other former slaveholding countries are understood, their consequences are not too surprising.

Past advantages achieved by American whites in the United States and elsewhere cannot be addressed successfully, let alone remedied, simply by ignoring them and creating a scenario of free market competition.

The consequence of this state of affairs is all too clear in the United States today and is perhaps most apparent in the simple fact of life itself: African American males in the United States can expect to live to the age of 71.7 (National Vital Statistics System, 2017), whereas white males can expect to live about five years longer. In no way can any policy based on "color-blindness" or "abstract liberalism" address, let alone remedy, this entrenched situation.

Peace cannot be achieved until justice is done—and justice requires the undoing of past wrongs to the point where the economic opportunities, as well as the symbolic status of those treated unfairly in the past are restored. While not all contemporaries are guilty of racism and discrimination, we all are responsible for undoing the conditions that have perpetuated inequality, unfairness, and unequal opportunities. Recognition and restitution are the *sine qua non* conditions for justice, fairness, and equal opportunity. A competition is fair only if we all start from the same place, and only if we are all equipped with the same resources (Rawls, 2001). The biggest impediment to achieving such an establishment of justice is not the population that would benefit from it but rather the population that has benefited over centuries from historic opportunity hoarding (Tilly, 1998).

Past privilege is sticky and tends to work cumulatively. It is also of a compound nature in that the starting position one holds vis-à-vis others becomes a decisive factor in determining future positions and hierarchies. In all former slave societies of the Americas, white America invested into its own future for 300 years before black America was allowed to make the first deposit.

African Americans are thus forced to live in a paradoxical world, where, on the surface, "everybody is equal" and has equal opportunities, while in most competitions centered on such scarce opportunities as jobs, housing, and education, they constantly seem to lose: the data on wealth could not be more telling. African American families hold less than 6 percent of the average wealth of white American families (Dettling et al., 2017). Wealth, which often emanates from assets acquired in overtly racist markets and subsequently passed down across generations, in turn opens the doors to better housing, in more affluent neighborhoods, with better schools—thus perpetuating the cycle. African Americans live in a society that blames them for not succeeding as a group and for not advancing toward those goals that make up the American Dream. Insult is thus added to injustice. What must be done?

LEARNING FROM JEWS AND GERMANS: RECOGNITION, REPARATIONS, AND CONFISCATION OF RICHES ACCUMULATED THROUGH SLAVE LABOR

The atrocities the German state and its people committed against Jews can hardly be overstated—and yet in 2006, when Germany hosted the soccer World Cup, German flags and other symbols of German nationalism, hitherto associated with Nazism, had apparently lost their Nazi connotation. Germans, for the most part, are able to interact with Jews without shame and guilt—some sixty years after the end of the Holocaust.

Germany, in other words, has at least partially achieved what the United States has failed to accomplish: an overcoming of past crimes and atrocities and a reestablishment of networks of mutual engagement, even trust, among the formerly enslaved and their oppressors (Neiman, 2019). Today, Germans can interact with German and other Jews in their middle without feeling ashamed, or guilty—while interactions between American whites and blacks often remain awkward. How was Germany able to do that?

By 1944, 26.5 percent of the nation's workforce consisted of foreigners who were forced to work for the German Reich. In 2000, the German government, in cooperation with six partner organizations from Russia, Ukraine, Belarus, Poland, and the Czech Republic, along with the Jewish Claims Conference, created the foundation *Erinnerung, Verantwortung und Zukunft* (Remembrance, Responsibility, and Future). Through it, reparation payments were made until June 2007:

> Former slave labourers [received] as much as DM15,000 (7,669.38 Euros) each, in two installments. In all, between the first payouts in June 2001 and the end of the programme in June 2007, some 4.37 billion Euros was paid to about 1.66 million beneficiaries in 100 countries. (von Plato, Leh, and Thonfeld, 2010: 8)

As early as 1943, Georg Landauer, "an influential German Zionist living in Palestine" (Balabkins, 1971: 82), argued for the right of Jews as a nation to press claims against Germany. Siegfried Moses, the "future comptroller of the State of Israel" (Balabkins, 1971: 82), published concrete proposals on how to implement such reparations. Nehemiah Robinson, then the head of the Institute of Jewish Affairs of the World Jewish Congress, was the first to put a concrete amount to the amount of reparations owed by Germany to the Jews: 12 billion German marks. In a letter to the Allied powers on September 20, 1945, Chaim Weizmann, the first president of Israel, calculated Jewish losses to Nazi Germany at 8 billion German marks: "Dr. Weizmann requested that all buildings, art treasures, and valuables of every kind be restored to their former owners or their heirs. All property for which no heirs could be traced was to be turned over to the Jewish Agency for Palestine, as the official representative of the Jews" (Balabkins, 1971: 84). Later, Weizmann calculated the amount to be paid out to survivors, their descendants, and their representatives at £2 billion— a sum amounting to £71 trillion to £390 trillion in today's value.[2]

Against the often violent protests of those who did not want to accept blood money from the Germans, Israeli leader David Ben-Gurion and German chancellor Konrad Adenauer (1949–63), who also faced opposition from various German constituents, were able to agree on the payment of reparations. Balabkins reports, "The Germans agreed to pay between DM 3.4 and 3.5 billion; agreement was also reached on the annual payments, including the obligation to deliver goods in the amount of DM 400 million before March 31, 1954" (1971: 134).

On September 10, 1952, the Federal Republic of Germany, now recognized by the Western states as a sovereign country (in breach of the Potsdam Agreement, signed after the war's end, and thus without the recognition of the Soviet Union), signed the Restitution Agreement in Luxembourg. Israel had by then settled on a claim amount of US$1.5 billion. Against the resistance of many members of Parliament, Adenauer stood with Israel. The resulting treaty was ratified in the German Bundestag in March 1953, and imbursement started soon thereafter. In fact, between 1953 and 1967, Germany paid Israel the total established amount of DM 3 billion, as well as DM 450 million to the Jewish Congress.

The Jewish state invested the money mostly in the country's infrastructure. Israel bought equipment and raw materials for the emerging, publicly controlled Israeli industries. Israel updated its electrical grid and invested about half of the incoming money into railways. Mining equipment and water canalization infrastructure were also high on the list of priorities, as were buying fuel and investing in commercial ships. "During the twelve years the reparations agreement was in effect, Israel's gross national product tripled; the Bank of Israel reckoned that 15 percent of this growth, and 45,000 jobs, could be attributed to investments made with reparation monies" (Segev, 1991: 241).

Germany, as well as Austria, also addressed the specific situation of slave labor during the Third Reich. Some twelve million people were forced to work for the Nazis in slave-like conditions—sometimes to their deaths. In 2000, the German government established the *Remembrance, Responsibility, and the Future* Foundation for the specific purpose of paying reparations to all those who suffered as slave or forced laborers under the Third Reich. A report to the US Congress, issued by the Bureau of European and Eurasian Affairs in March 2006, states:

> The United States Government played a critical role in a multilateral effort that resulted in the establishment of a Foundation under German law entitled "Remembrance, Responsibility, and the Future" ("Foundation"). The Foundation was capitalized with 10 billion German Marks (DM), valued at the time as approximately five billion dollars. Since June 2001, the Foundation has been making payments to survivors in recognition of the suffering they endured as slave and forced laborers. The Foundation also covers other personal inquiry and certain property damage caused by German companies during the Nazi era, including claims against German banks and insurance companies. (Bureau of European and Eurasian Affairs, 2006)

The same report explains, "As of December 2005, approximately $5.1 billion (4.265 billion Euro or 8.3 billion DM) had been paid to approximately 1,646,000 surviving slave and forced laborers."

Indeed, the official *Agreement between the Government of the United States of America and the Government of the Federal Republic of Germany concerning the Foundation "Remembrance, Responsibility and the Future"* states:

> The Foundation legislation will provide that persons who were held in concentration camps as defined under the Federal Compensation Law ("BEG") or another place of confinement or ghetto under comparable conditions and were subject to forced labor ("slave laborers") will be eligible to receive up to DM 15,000 each [...] The eligibility of all laborers covered by the Foundation will be limited to survivors and heirs as defined under paragraph 8, of those who died after February 15, 1999 [...]
>
> 7. The Foundation legislation, by making available the amount of 50 million DM, will provide a potential remedy for all non-racially motivated wrongs of German companies directly resulting in loss of or damage to property during the National Socialist era [...]
>
> 8. The Foundation legislation will provide that the heirs eligible to receive payments under paragraphs 6 and 7 consist of the spouse or children. In the absence of the victim, spouse and children, then payments under these paragraphs will be available to grandchildren, if alive; if not, to siblings, if alive; and if there are neither grandchildren not siblings, to the individual beneficiary named in a will.
>
> 9. The Foundation legislation will provide that all eligibility decisions will be based on relaxed standards of proof. (*Agreement* 2000, annex A)

The monies paid through the *Remembrance, Responsibility, and the Future* Foundation between 2000 and 2007 were not the end, however, of German atonement for genocide and enslavement. In 2009, Israeli finance minister Yuval Steinitz demanded €450 million to €1 billion in pension payments from Germany on behalf of Jews forced into slave labor during the Holocaust. Israeli officials referred to the "ghetto workers act" (Gesetz zur Zahlbarmachung von Renten aus Beschäftigungen in einem Ghetto, Deutscher Bundestag, 2002), passed by the German parliament in 2002, and calculated that the 30,000 living survivors of forced labor were entitled to a retroactive payment of approximately €15,000 each (Bassok and TheMarker, 2009). In 2013, Germany agreed to pay US $1 billion for the home care of elderly Holocaust survivors worldwide.

In 2014, the German Bundestag finally agreed to pay all those forced to work in Nazi ghettos retroactive pensions, reaching back to 1997 (Claims Conference, 2014).

Moreover, in April 2015, 93-year-old Oscar Gröning went on trial in Lüneburg, Germany, accused of participating in the murder of 300,000 Jews in Auschwitz-Birkenau (Smale, 2015). Gröning thus became one of the last living Nazis to finally face trial for the crimes they committed, or were complicit with, against Jews, socialists, Roma, communists, homosexuals, and conscientious objectors. He was prosecuted 70 years after the crimes—and yet, as I argue here, it was not too late. It is, in fact, never too late to address the wrongs committed in the past for the sake of establishing justice today.

Reparations, however, only represented one side of the actions taken to atone for the Holocaust and for the enslavement of thousands. Postwar Germany also addressed the other side of the coin: the riches accumulated through theft and slavery. In fact, the Allied forces already agreed in 1943 to return the riches stolen by the Nazis. In 1947, the American forces in Germany passed law No. 59 to return the riches stolen from the victims of Nazim to their rightful owners. The British and French forces soon followed suit. Law No. 59 was later integrated into the new German constitution, as article 11 remains a part of the German constitution to this day.

Companies employing slave laborers, such as IG Farben, Krupp and Flick were dismantled by the Allied forces. During the Subsequent Nuremberg Military Trials, their directors were convicted of war crimes. They were found guilty of crimes against humanity for using hundreds of thousands of enslaved laborers during the Nazi regime.

While the dismantling of riches accumulated through slave labor under the Nazis was not thorough enough and incomplete, it nevertheless set an important precedence and signal. The riches accumulated by enslaved people belong to them, not to their enslavers. Justice demands that those riches are dismantled and either returned to their rightful owners from whom they have been stolen or distributed among those who made them possible.

It is, in this regard, worth mentioning that France has received reparations for their loss of property, that is slaves, from independent Haiti. Haiti made such payments to France until 1947, paying a total of US $21 billion, in current value (Sommers, 2015). When Haitian then-president Aristide demanded reparations from France, in 2003, France not only denied any payments but it also blocked sending UN peacekeepers to Haiti until after sitting president Aristide was removed from power by a coup. Germany also did not extend the same treatment to others who suffered under the Nazi regime. Sinti and Roma groups have unsuccessfully sought recognition and reparations from Germany for the crimes committed against them, and the same is true for LGBTI individuals.

Germany did not recognize the genocide it committed on the Herero and Nama people between 1904 and 1905 in today's Namibia. Adenauer, who issued the official apology for the Holocaust in 1951, in fact served as the vice president of the German Colonial Society during the 1930s and lobbied for Germany to get back its African colonies after losing all of them at Versailles, in 1919, in the aftermath of World War I (Perraudin and Zimmerer, 2010; Hansen and Jonson, 2014). As a whole, therefore, Germany is not a model country in regard to atoning for past crimes. The Jewish case in particular, however, offers valuable lessons for other cases where past injustices have not been adequately addressed—including those concerning the Herero and Nama, as well as the Sinti, Roma, and LGBTI victims of German Nazism.

Reparations, as I have hoped to show, are much more than individual compensation for damages and crimes committed. They are an integral part of atonement, and as such, they can play an important role in supporting communities that have suffered injustice. The German case shows that atonement is possible. It also shows that reparations need to not only address those who have been harmed but those who unduly benefitted must also be targeted with expropriation measures. Fairness demands measures for both— the formerly enslaved and the former enslavers to set things right and to create equal opportunities and justice unburdened by the legacies of the past.

The investments into Israel helped the emerging Jewish community to grow strong and independent. It allowed for the success of an emerging nation-state, able to decide how to best educate, and defend, its own. It contributed to Jewish efforts to free itself from the legacies of Nazism by promoting its own language, its own educational institutions, and its own defense. The Jewish post-Holocaust program thus bears much resemblance to some African American proposals aimed at achieving more autonomy, protection, health, and education—for example, those formulated by the Black Panthers, who demand, in their Ten-Point Program:

1. We want freedom. We want power to determine the destiny of our Black Community.
2. We want full employment for our people.
3. We want an end to the robbery by the white men of our Black Community (later changed to "we want an end to the robbery by the capitalists of our black and oppressed communities").
4. We want decent housing, fit for shelter of human beings.

5. We want education for our people that exposes the true nature of this decadent American society. We want education that teaches us our true history and our role in the present-day society.
6. We want all black men to be exempt from military service.
7. We want an immediate end to **POLICE BRUTALITY** and **MURDER** of black people.
8. We want freedom for all black men held in federal, state, county, and city prisons and jails.
9. We want all black people when brought to trial to be tried in court by a jury of their peer group or people from their Black Communities, as defined by the Constitution of the United States.
10. We want land, bread, housing, education, clothing, justice and peace.

Germany, however, had lost a war and former Nazi leaders were forced to stand trial. Jewish organizations, such as the World Jewish Congress, the Institute on Jewish Affairs/Jewish Policy Research, the American Jewish History Society, as well as several Jewish foundations and federations played an important role in pressing forward with claims and ensuring that the Holocaust would not be forgotten. Collective memory and official history had to be rewritten to ensure that the Holocaust would be remembered. Recognition thus was and continued to be an important component of atonement.

RECOGNITION

In addition to reparations, the German state also invested in recognition of the evils done in the past, promoting "Vergangenheitsaufarbeitung," literally working through the past, so that one can move on, or work up from the past to construct the present. In Germany, the Criminal Code, paragraph 86a, outlaws the use of symbols of unconstitutional organizations. In 1968, this code was amended to prohibit the preparation of a war of aggression and the incitement of war (paragraphs 80 and 80a), the dissemination of means of propaganda of unconstitutional organizations (paragraph 80), the usage of symbols of unconstitutional organizations (paragraph 86a), and the incitement of hatred against segments of the population (paragraph 130). With this, the usage or display of any symbol related to Nazism was outlawed, punishable with up to three years of imprisonment. In Germany as well as in Austria, which has adopted similar laws, this means that nobody can raise their arm in the Nazi salute or display a swastika. Hitler's book *Mein Kampf* was unavailable for sale in both nations until 2016, when it entered the public domain. While Germans and Austrians value free speech just as much as Americans, in Germany and Austria, the line separating free speech from hate speech are drawn differently. Recognizing hate speech for what it is has become a pillar of these European democracies, as it allows for the protection of segments of its societies against the vicious attacks by other segments and the harm, both physical and emotional, such attacks can do.

The German state, even if reluctantly and too late for many and at times against internal opposition, has at least partially faced the evil it did to Jews. This has allowed Germans of the postwar generation to look upon Jews and Israel without guilt. Even more importantly, it has allowed contemporary Germans to look upon themselves as no longer burdened with a past of crime and exploitation. Germans today travel to Israel and are welcomed there. They attend Israeli universities. Jewish people again live in such cities as Berlin, which is home to some forty thousand Jews.

This is due, in my assessment, precisely because a past of atrocities and genocide was not simply forgotten. Instead, it was addressed, "worked through," and elevated to a defining characteristic of post–World War II Germany. As Susan Neiman (2019) so eloquently shows, this "Vergangenheitsaufarbeitung," or "working through" the past opened the doors for a gradual, if painful, normalization. Most postwar Germans know of their historical guilt and many feel a special responsibility toward achieving justice everywhere because of it. My own generation (I was born in West Germany in 1968) was profoundly marked by this past, which made most of us uneasy to stand to the German flag or sing the German national hymn. I, myself, have never done so in my life—and I was never required to do so. We were still too close to National Socialism for such displays to be perceived, and accepted, as normal and acceptable.

It is with this background in mind that the return to a normal display of German flags, which occurred for the first time in postwar history during the World Cup Soccer in 2006, was so remarkable. Many Germans of my generations did not feel personally guilty of the Nazi crimes, but we felt responsible to make sure nothing like Nazism could ever emerge again. Many among us also felt responsible to stand up against genocide, abuse, enslavement, and other injustices wherever they occurred. Post–World War II German school children, me included, did not learn much, if at all, about reparations Germany paid to Israel. But we did learn about the Holocaust and we were aware about the laws making the display of hate symbols illegal. Recognition, for us, was the main way to overcome guilt and achieve normalcy. And it was the way to educate many post–World War II Germans into becoming anti-fascists, anti-racists, and anti-war activists.

More than official laws and regulation, it was the young protest generation of 1968 who questioned the values and practices inherited from the Nazi past in Germany through many acts of protest and civil disobedience. West Germany demanded military service from its male citizens from 1956 to 2011. The number of conscientious objectors, who refused to join the military and offered to conduct social service instead steadily rose in West Germany from under 6,000 until 1968 to 11,952 in that year. In 1977, almost seventy thousand applications were filed, reaching 151,212 in 1991. Anti-militarism thus took time to blossom in West Germany.

Similarly, the by now much-noted initiative to install stumble stones, bearing the name and date of assassination of Jewish people in Europe created by the German artist Gunter Deming, also only started in the early 2000s. Since then, over twelve hundred such commemorative plates have been laid down in front of the houses and appartments of former Jewish residents.

Atonement takes time, but it must start with an admission of guilt and a taking of responsibility for those unduly harmed. Recognition must lead to a rewriting of history and a raising of awareness of what exactly happened to the victims of injustice, as well as to those who took advantage of them. Recognition must thus be followed by education. To be affective, reparations in the form of structural community investments in health, education, jobs, and property- and wealth-building institutions must follow. Israel provides the best empirical example of what investment in a minority community can achieve, as Israel started to write, and control, its own history after the Holocaust.

African Americans and formerly enslaved people everywhere can certainly extract important lessons from the case of Israel—even if statehood might not be the solution they seek. Safety, prosperity, and control over one's own destiny, however, still eludes most descendants of formerly enslaved people. Official histories still deny their roles in the creation of modern nations and the riches accumulated through slavery are still not controlled by those who made them possible. Reconstruction was only tried in the United States, where it failed miserably. Such countries like Brazil, Colombia, Cuba, and others, most of which looking back at a history of enslaving many more people than the United States, never even tried to reconstruct after slavery ended.

TRUTH IN THE UNITED STATES

Historian Eric Foner (2014) has argued that after the Civil War, white Americans did not only refuse to apologize for slavery, but they also refused to accept former slaves as equals and thus perpetuated their stigmatization, excluding them from their concept of a shared humanity. As Anthony Marx (1998) demonstrates, instead of apologizing and allowing African Americans to become part of their community, southern whites demanded legal segregation as a condition of remaining in the Union. Racist white southerners and the northern allies not only refused to apologize and to accept blacks as equals, but they also ended reconstruction efforts and then reversed even the tiny achievements that the US Bureau of Refugees, Freedmen, and Abandoned Land was able to obtain for them in the early days after the war (Foner, 2014). What, then, is the truth in the United States?

The story for the United States is different from that of Nazi Germany. Here, too, white supremacists have enslaved, killed, and exploited. Africans and their descendants were brought to the Americas against their will. Slaveholders and their descendants accumulated riches on plantations, farms, and industries built on free and later very cheap black labor. Whites forced enslaved people to construct mansions still seen today in the US South. Despite desegregation laws, residential segregation to this day follows the pattern established hundreds of years ago.

In contrast to Germany's ban on Nazi symbols, white Southerners proudly parade the Confederate flag. Mississippi has the Confederate emblem integrated in its state flag. The state flag of Alabama looks much like the Confederate flag—just without the stars. Florida's also does not display much variation from the original Confederate flag from which it took inspiration. To this day, it is common to encounter belts, stickers, and license plates proudly displaying the Confederate flag. Nobody doing so is in any sort of legal jeopardy; they seem to feel safe, not fearing reprisal either from the state or from outraged citizens. After all, the law is on their side. Thus, in the United States, recognition for African Americans failed—and continues to fail them.

Reconstruction failed. The US Bureau of Refugees, Freedmen, and Abandoned Land was created in 1865 to support the formerly enslaved, after the US South had lost its right to enslave others, but it was closed again by Congress in 1872 (Foner 2002). Moreover, instead of providing land to former slaves, President Andrew Johnson issued pardons to Confederates restoring their land titles (Foner, 2002: 159), and, therefore, the 40 acres that the bureau intended to give to every freedman from public land never materialized. Instead, the land that had been given to former slaves was given back to its previous owners. According to Foner (2002: 159), probably the most eminent contemporary historian of the Reconstruction era, "Once growing crops had been harvested, virtually all the land in Bureau hands would revert to its former owners."

Leveling the playing field and establishing equal opportunities for all would have required not only giving land to blacks so they could sustain themselves but also taking away those riches accumulated by whites during and because of slavery, particularly on plantations. However, even though Congress passed the Confiscation Act in 1862, President Lincoln steered against its large-scale implementation, limiting the tenure of confiscated land to one generation so that the land would eventually revert to its original owners. According to Foner (2002: 51), "The President had no enthusiasm for large-scale confiscation that, he feared, would undermine efforts to win the support of loyal planters and other Southern whites, and the act remained largely unenforced."

What stood in the way of a genuine end to inequality was racism. Foner (2002: 150) quotes Colonel Samuel Thomas, the director of the Mississippi Bureau of Reconstruction in 1865, who thought "the basic problem [...] was that the white public could not conceive of the negro having any rights at all."

Literacy among slaves had been against the law in several states including Mississippi, Virginia, and South Carolina, and after the end of the Civil War, only a few black colleges opened their doors, providing higher education to a tiny minority of former slaves and their descendants. In 1896, the US Supreme Court confirmed the "separate but equal" doctrine, which justified legal segregation and perpetuated substandard education, health, and housing facilities for nonwhites. African Americans continued to be discriminated against in the labor market, the education market, and the mortgage market.

In his Pulitzer Prize–winning book *Slavery by Another Name*, Douglas Blackmon (2008) has carefully documented how slavery was perpetuated in the United States until the 1950s, as African Americans fell victim to false accusations (like "vagrancy") and were then traded to work off their prison sentence in the mines, woods, and plantations of Alabama, Georgia, Mississippi, Texas, and other former Confederate States. Northern industries, such as American Steel, were involved in these widespread schemes and profited from them. Blackmon (2009) documents that the FBI, created in 1908, and its predecessors, as well as other federal agencies, knew about the effective practice of slavery in the American South and refused to take action.

Black farmers were excluded from the state-sponsored land grant universities emerging after 1862, providing the state support needed to allow white farmers to embark on an unprecedented agricultural expansion and the modernization of American farming. Social security, created in response to the Great Depression under Franklin D. Roosevelt's New Deal, excluded farm and domestic workers also until the 1950s, thus disproportionally affecting African Americans. To this day, farm workers are not allowed to unionize, their vulnerability perpetuated.

Even after the 1950s, African Americans suffered from discriminatory housing and lending practices, thus blocking their access to homeownership and to "good," that is affluent white, neighborhoods—a practice known as "redlining." Homeownership and education were severely impacted by these discriminatory policies and practices, as living in poor school district automatically translates into receiving poor education, leading to lower job opportunities, lower income, and so on.

The latest in this ongoing history of discrimination affecting African Americans disproportionally were the laws resulting from Regan's "war against drugs" unduly differentiating between different usages of cocaine and targeting mostly urban poor African Americans. Incarceration policies and practices, to this day, target and affect African Americans disproportionally, thus perpetuating their disadvantages, particularly vis-à-vis white and Asian Americans.

The usage of racist symbols is to this day supported by the "free speech" protection clause, as written in the First Amendment to the Constitution, ratified in 1791. Instead of receiving reparations and land, former slaves witnessed the emergence of the Ku Klux Klan in 1865. By the 1920s, the Klan counted four million members and operated in almost every state. Instead of seeing the riches they helped accumulate taken away from their former masters and distributed among them, freed men and women found themselves without land, without shelter, and without access to quality education or quality health care. They witnessed the passing of vagrancy laws that demonized them and sought to push them out of cities. In short, Reconstruction failed on all levels, both symbolic and material.

This reality is particularly sobering when considering the fact that the US government played such a critical role in the process of securing reparations for slave laborers in Germany. The United States, of course, was also the driving force behind the Nuremberg trials and the prosecution of Nazi criminals and the expropriation of all those enriching themselves through slave labor.

While supporting reparations for the victims of the Nazis, the US legislature has been unwilling to do the same with the descendants of the over four million slaves in the United States at the end of the Civil War. In fact, a bill seeking to establish a committee to study slavery and its effects and elaborate the appropriate measures to undo the harms it did has been proposed every year since 1989 by Congressman John Conyers Jr. until his retirement in 2017, but it never became a law.

It is also worth considering that while most American countries of the American hemisphere did not erect such severe and overtly racist institutions and attitudes as whites did in the United States, most of them practiced slavery much longer. Brazil enslaved 10 times as many Africans as the United States and it did so much longer—from the 1530s to at least 1888. Colombia, Peru, Argentina, Chile, and other South American countries all started enslavement in the early to mid-sixteenth century and practiced it until the early or mid-nineteenth century. In the Caribbean, slavery changed an entire demographics, eradicating the native population and forcefully introducing over five million enslaved Africans who make up the majority population there to this day. Racism and the systematic exploitation of Native Americans and Africans and their descendants *were* the foundations upon which modern American societies were erected.

CONCLUSIONS

Reparations cannot undo guilt. Achieving this would require understanding and accepting the fact that white privilege was constructed in the United States on the backs of black people and to their detriment. This can only occur if white Americans are made to understand not only their own privileges but also the continued stigmatization that African Americans experience every day—and its consequences. One way to achieve this is through education. US schools—from kindergarten to high school—must teach how white privilege is constructed and perpetuated and how blacks continue to be stigmatized. History would have to be taught in different ways, recognizing black contributions and white exploitation; US nationalism would have to be changed to acknowledge the injustices inflicted upon African Americans and Native Americans so that they can then be imagined as full and equal members of the US community from which they are currently excluded. *Vergangenheitsaufarbeitung* would have to occur.

After a collective admission of guilt in the form of changed school curriculums and an altered US nationalism, action must follow in the form of reparations. The historical gap that separates current generations from slaveholders might seem wide, but the benefits from past racial injustice are all too visible today.

Justice demands not simply recognition but equal opportunities. Unless the playing field is level for all, free competition will not offset the wrongdoings that structured the field in the past—especially in a situation where one group of players has been systematically stigmatized and denied access to the status of full and shared humanity. Affirmative action, together with the Equal Employment Opportunity Commission established by the Civil Rights Act of 1964, have certainly enabled some nonwhites to find decent work as well as gain some access to selective institutions of higher education (Bowen and Bok, 2000). Affirmative action policies, however, have been far too limited and specific to achieve justice. Justice must be constructed on equal opportunity, and equal opportunity has to be created—and enforced—*before* people compete against each other, as even Rawls (2001), the godfather of individual liberalism, admits. For the United States to achieve racial justice, the lessons from Germany are invaluable:

1. All symbols glorifying racism should be classified as hate speech and outlawed;
2. The riches accumulated during slavery and through slave labor should be confiscated from their current owners and given to the descendants of those who actually constructed them and then suffered from the legacies of slavery; and
3. Black institutions, infrastructure, and organizations should be massively supported by the state, using the resources repossessed from slaveholding. These institutions include infrastructure, health, education, and transportation of predominantly black neighborhoods, historically black colleges, and predominantly black schools and kindergartens.

Achieving these goals would, of course, pose logistical difficulties, but the principles under which German reparations were paid must be upheld: those individuals and their descendants who benefited directly from slavery must be identified, and the worth of their possessions must be assessed and traced to the present day. Those who were enslaved have to be identified along with their descendants and they should be compensated and offered institutional support that allow them to prosper.

While there has been considerable debate about the pragmatism of paying reparations today, as well as much controversy about the technical aspects of doing so (Torpey, 2017; Ogletree, 2004; Dalby, 2002; Dawson, 2002; Reed, 2000; R. Robinson, 2000; Brooks, 1999; Bell, 1987, 1974; Bittker, [1973] 2003; Darity and Mullen, 2020), in this chapter I have argued that addressing the disadvantages affecting one group at the hands of another is a requirement if justice and moral reconciliation are the goals. While implementation may pose difficulties, paying reparations and recognizing that white privilege was constructed at black expense must be seen as the sine qua non condition to achieve justice and undo age-old guilt.

CHAPTER 5

CONCLUSIONS AND IMPLICATIONS

For the sake of fairness and equal opportunity, we have to limit the things that money can buy. It is not fair if some can spend thousands on college prep courses, while others have to take college entrance exams without being able to prepare for them adequately. It is not fair that some universities have so much money that they can support their students' research while others cannot. It is not fair that the rich have formed clubs to support each other's businesses, while those who cannot afford to join are left to fend for themselves. It is not fair that only the rich can get elected to public office and it is not fair that some political candidates can draw on millions of dollars to influence elections. It is not fair that the rich have reserved all the beach houses and, it appears, the whole of real estate of California, for themselves. It is not fair that those who inherited millions can make a living simply by investing their money in the stock market. The word "earning" does not even apply here, as there is no effort made, no responsibility taken, no sweat broken. For the sake of fairness and equal opportunity, we either all have to work, or none of us have to, in order to make a living.

While abolishing competition altogether has proven hazardous, limiting competition and establishing the background conditions for fairness and equal opportunity has not been tried. It is, however, the most promising strategy I can think of.

Markets can be anything we collectively, and politically decide them to be. Our most ardent task today is to look for ways to curb the undue influence of a few rich individuals and groups or corporations onto the political process. This is not to say that our main strategy must be to cut back on government, as the libertarian fraction argues. Their arguments do not aim at improving governance, let alone democracy, but at providing free license to entrepreneurs in hopes that somehow, miraculously, more capitalism will fix it, where "it" includes, in their account, justice, fairness, and equal opportunity (Doherty, 2008). There is, however, not one good reason to assume that, but a myriad of evidence on how unrestrained capitalism does just the opposite (Harvey, 2011). We must, in short, find ways to ensure and protect that ordinary citizens can have a say in the kind of laws and rules they have to live under. Political apathy and alienation can only be fought back when and if ordinary citizens know and feel that they have something at stake in politics. The direction of reform therefore must necessarily be one that brings the state and government back to the people. Doing so bears the promise of also reigning in the economy, bringing it back under the control of the many by taking it away from the authority of those powerful actors that have been able to escape the control of the collective.

While the concentration of wealth is perceived by some as morally degrading in itself, others focus on its moral effects on the larger community, or on its potential to spill over into politics. Wealth leads to more wealth—that is the core insight driving all these debates. Wealth also leads to a hoarding of opportunities in that economic wealth easily translates into other realms and provides those entering competitive markets with large assets with undue advantages. These advantages are ultimately unjustifiable. To others, this is not a question or morals, but of fair competition, or even economic efficiency. From Adam Smith to James Meade, Samuel Bowles and Herbert Gintis (1998) and Fred Hirsch (1976), economists have highlighted the dangers of monopolies—a tendency greatly enhanced by high asset concentrations. If a small group of people—let's say the richest 1 percent of adults who, according to Oxfam (January 2015), own 50 percent of the world's wealth—has already brought most goods and assets under their control—then these goods and assets are no longer on the market for the 99 percent who are not rich. The 99 percent, as a result, have to complete on a market that is not only reduced by 50 percent. It is also a market where all the most desirable goods and assets have already been bought up and are shielded against the competition of the 99 percent through high prices.

Concretely, this means that the vast majority of average earning people will never gain access to houses on the beach, or to apartments in New York City, London, Frankfurt, or Hong Kong. Nor will they ever gain systematic access to high quality education. Never—unless those goods are reintroduced back into the market of average-earning citizens.

The very broad spectrum of authors discussed here represent only a small fraction of authors and average people who have reached the same, apparently inevitable conclusion: to protect equal opportunity and fairness while also protecting against tyrannical states and their apparatuses, asset holding has to be limited; asset inheritance has to be radically undermined; education and health services have to be made available to all in the same way and with the same quality. Those who press this further, like John Rawls, Amartya Sen, and Brian Barry have argued that those who enter competitive situations with a disadvantage need to receive more assets and education so they can reach a position of equal opportunity *before* they start competing with everybody else. These conclusions are inevitable if democracy, fairness, and equal opportunity are the goals. These proposals are, as I have hoped to demonstrate, not radical or utopian, but practical and realistic in their necessity.

I am unaware of any current concrete proposals to enact upper limits of income and wealth possession, other than in Bolivia. This topic is, however, of the utmost importance and central to any attempt to protect equal opportunity and fairness, as I hope to have demonstrated. While discussing minimum wages has much merit, a much more important and urgent discussion we need to have is about maximum wages and, even more importantly, maximum asset holdings, be it in the form of land, real estate, securities, or any other form of asset.

How to enact such policies and what sort of specific policy proposals promise the most efficient way to control and counteract high asset concentration should become one of the core discussions of any democracy concerned about fairness and equal opportunity. In its absence, war and destruction provide the only mechanisms able to level the playfield for future generations. So far, most Western societies have relied precisely on those destructive forces to provide the young with new opportunities (Schumpeter, 1976). As a result, most postwar societies experienced growth and opportunities. Death and destruction thus allowed for new opportunities and space for expansion for those who survived. We cannot, however, wait on the destructive forces of war, nature, or capitalism to provide new generations of people with economic opportunities. Or maybe, we should not. Asset limitations, coupled with high quality, universal education and high quality health care make it possible to entrust new generations to themselves and their communities—without having to provide them with unfair privileges so they can prevail over all others. Such a model is not sustainable on the long run, as not all can win and even if a few win due to their inherited privileges, the majority will always lose.

For democracy to work, the logic of stakeholdership must be applied. Citizens must be actively involved in the practical and routine running and execution of democracy. Democracy is the people's system, not a system where some people can take over the practice and execution of democracy for others and rule over them. The liberal dream of reaping all the benefits from democracy while not contributing to it at all has turned into a true nightmare. To end it, we must end elite rule and take on active roles as active citizens.

I have shown, in the chapters above, what a paradigm shift in the social science can achieve: once we let go of the old paradigms of political presentation, redistribution, and focusing exclusively on the lower end of the wealth spectrum when designing social policies, new perspectives and possibilities become apparent. Sortition and legal duty, predistribution, reparations, and upper limits to wealth and asset holding emerge as possibilities.

At this point in the debate, they are just that: possibilities. We currently lack the practical knowledge and the experience to fully grasp the impact of such policies and the societal and environmental changes they are likely to produce. Without new paradigms, thinking about such new possibilities is rendered impossible and no systematic knowledge about them can be accumulated. I hope that this book contributes to establishing these new paradigms so that others can follow up and we can all try out better ways to protect fairness, equal opportunity, and environmental soundness. The implications and promises of adapting these new paradigms are manifold. They include:

POLITICS INVIGORATED

If citizens could make important political and economic decisions about local politics that is at the town, city, or in large cities, the neighborhood level, through direct democratic participation in town halls and participatory budgeting schemes, politics would be greatly invigorated. Through their participation, citizens would learn the "art of politics" and become political beings—zoon politicon. The many studies of participative budgeting and participative planning have shown that average people are willing to participate as long as their participation has tangible results. New England town halls only meet once a year, thus keeping the demand of hours and efforts to a very manageable minimum. Participatory budgeting does not necessarily require personal presence, as much or the participation with regards to sorting out preferences can be done online, along the lines developed by crowd sourcing approach, developed by Beth Noveck and her NYU Governance Lab.

The main requirement for local direct democracy is that localities have the power and the money to decide for themselves. Local direct democracy thus requires decentralization and federalism beyond what most countries have today, shifting decision-making and budgeting authority down to the local level.

Such countries as Canada and Denmark already have highly decentralized political systems. In Canada, almost 80 percent of public expenditures are done by subnational governments, thus demonstrating that decentralization is possible, under certain conditions (such as investment in and training of local bureaucrats). The next step for already highly decentralized countries consists of democratizing the political decision-making processes by opening it up to average citizens. Here, Vermont and Switzerland can both serve as models of how to achieve that.

At the national, transnational, and international levels, having randomly selected citizens meet once a year to deliberate and decide about new laws would provide an opportunity for average citizens to get to know how and for whom government and lawmaking actually work. In such large countries as the United States, legal duty could be restricted to once-a-lifetime public service and it could be combined with spending three days in Washington, DC and getting to know not just the nation's capital, but also its different political, legislative, and juridical institutions. Here the formulas and experience that James Fishkin and his team have acquired over the years when applying "deliberative polls" could serve as the model to follow. If conducted that way, up to 300 people or more, from all across the country, randomly selected, could meet, receive expert information, and, divided into smaller groups of up to 15, could debate the merits of a legal initiative or bill.

Local direct democracy, combined with a once-a-lifetime legal duty and the above-mentioned duty to vote in general elections, promises to bring politics back to the people.

LEARNING POLITICS THROUGH PRACTICE

Participation breeds more participation and participants become more politically savvy the more they participate. This is an old insight, but it still holds true today. Average citizens, in the kind of minimal, audience democracies of our days, do not know how to conduct politics. Politics requires compromise, willingness to listen to other, often divergent, opinions, and strategic thinking. It relies on forging alliances across different constituents. It involves oratorical skills and rhetoric. Professional politicians learn these skills on the job, and we witness how they become better and more skilled at their jobs the longer they serve in this capacity. However, as it is, professional politicians and the ruling class alone learn political skills and they shield average citizens from acquiring them.

Broad and regular active citizens participation promise to democratize political skills and know-how, spreading it across the entire population and thus contributing to political education at large. This seems particularly important for the youth, as today, young people are systematically excluded from acquiring political knowledge through practice—and yet they are the ones who inherit our world. Political involvement should start at an earlier age, maybe 16, like in Brazil, thus allowing for a political socialization of the youth and civic and political education should be a core curricular component of every democracy.

EXTREME VOICES SANCTIONED BY PUBLIC DELIBERATION

The kind of hate speech and often anonymous harassment of people who propose change cannot withstand public scrutiny. Open, public debate promises to weed out those opinions that are nasty and ill intended. If more citizens participated in public political debates with each other in heterogenous groups, then much of the fake news, exaggeration of difference and otherness, downplay of shared humanity, and bedeviling of other opinions would come to an end. After all, problems and difference take on greater dimensions in our imaginations if we are not exposed to those who hold different opinions and those who look different, or practice a different religion. Public deliberation at the local level, in direct democratic settings, but also serving on legal duty together promises to have a tempering effect on extremism by recognizing each other's humanity and value and, through it, the merit of other opinions. After all, it is precisely in those places with the least foreigners and immigrants that anti-immigrant and racist attitudes flourish the most. Here, too, practice and active involvement promise to teach average people the core political values of tolerance and compromise.

SPECIAL INTEREST POLITICS AND LOBBYING ENDED

If we put an end to electing politicians into public office, then a whole set of problems, all connected to voting and campaigning, would simply disappear. If average people, randomly selected, would get together occasionally to deliberate and pass new laws, then political campaigning would become a thing of the past, because nobody would know upfront for whom to lobby. The selection of deliberators should not be made public in advance so that those called upon would be shielded from public or private pressure. With such an arrangement, campaign contributions and all the other attempts to sway or convince professional politicians to pass laws in favor of those who give them money, gifts, or other rewards would also end, as nobody would know whom to pressure or persuade in advance. If lobbyist were not allowed in deliberative sessions, lobbying would come to an end in such a system. Interest groups would no longer know whom to target with their attempts to influence political decisions, so a political system reliant on lottery and sortition, combined with local direct democracy and town halls, would put an end to the influence of special interest, lobbying, and the undue influence of money in politics.

CORPORATE INFLUENCE ENDED

Along with ending the influence of lobbying and special interest groups, the current influence of powerful corporations in politics would also be curbed by a political system reliant on national sortition and local direct democracy. Just like lobbyist and special interest groups, corporations simply would not know whom to target with their political strategies and attempts to influence political outcomes—if people were randomly selected just for the occasion of coming together to deliberate.

MEDIA MANIPULATION ENDED

While the media would still play a large role in a sortition—deliberation political system, its role in producing fake news and hyping up differences and political scandals would be reduced, simply by the fact that average people would have more practical knowledge about politics and democracy. A culture of debate and deliberation would gradually emerge, replacing the current culture of manipulation and hyping of differences, and the media would have to follow this trend. To participate meaningfully locally and as national legislators, average citizens would require access to relevant political information, including budgets, and they would have to be able to find information on how government works. Under such a scenario, the political media will most likely experience a boost and a push toward more serious and informative coverage, and away from the sort of sensationalist headlining we have grown accustomed to over the past decades. After all, under the current paradigms, the media's main purpose seems to entertain and distract us from politics, whereas under the new paradigms I propose, its main function would change to informing citizens so they can be better prepared and equipped when called for legal duty.

INVIGORATED BUT FAIR COMPETITION WITH EQUAL OPPORTUNITIES

Reparations, combined with *predistribution* and the institution of *upper limits* to family wealth and income, would achieve several goals at once. Reparations are meant to create equal opportunities *before* people compete. If competitions are fair, then different people, with different characteristics will win at different times. Right now, those who can count on historical legacies, either in the form of inherited financial capital or in the form of inherited symbolic capitals win most competitions, most of the time. As a result of historically accumulated symbolic capital, white men win most competitions on most markets, most of the time, given the long-lasting results of racism and sexism—in those societies constructed on the bases of enslavement and European colonialism. Those able to rely on large financial inheritances, on the other hand, tend to win in most financial market competitions. Reparations promise to support those without historically accumulated financial and symbolic capitals, as these capitals tilt the playfield, making them unfair.

Predistribution aims at achieving the same goal as reparations but in a more general way and not specifically targeting the descendants of the formerly enslaved. If college education were free and those graduates without family wealth would receive a US $20,000 stipend upon successful graduation, then their chances of becoming successful entrepreneurs would greatly increase. Predistribution would invest in their individual capabilities and propel the agency of those who are held back from being successful because they lack the start-up funds. It would also compensate for the unequal situation we currently face, where those who can count on a rich family will not only leave college debt free but endowed with the necessary assets and connections (social capital) to create businesses. Such a policy would bring tremendous dynamism into markets and also have a tremendous impact on crime and incarceration rates, as it would provide opportunities to those who were born into them.

Upper limits, finally, would ensure that there are no billionaires among us and thus work against a reality where average people with average incomes can never win in most competitive scenarios we enter during our lives. Competition would be fairer. If we had no multimillionaires and billionaires, then all luxury assets would enter common markets and become available again to all of us. The superrich compete with each other in a market that is so expensive that average people can only read about it in the news. Upper limits promise to free up frozen assets and making them available again on general markets, thus greatly invigorating those general markets. Severe restriction on inheritance, as proposed above in combination with upper limits, would reintroduce frozen assets into general markets and make them available again and accessible to average buyers. Instead of relying on constant economic expansion and growth, such a system would come closer to the idea of recycling, as appropriated assets, instead of remaining outside of general markets and controlled by family dynasties, would reenter them and become available again, after the death of the owner.

RAMPANT ECONOMIC EXPANSION BLOCKED—AND ENVIRONMENT PROTECTED

Most market distortions happen at the extreme ends: excluded groups are forced out of markets and the extremely wealthy have found ways to shield their assets from open market competition through high price mechanisms. It is also clear what the general policies to combat this must achieve: they must push back the market capture of the rich and expand the market participation of the poor so that more people can effectively participate with equal opportunities, that is, fairly.

It is also clear that any attempt at creating fairer markets, or markets that are more embedded in local communities and subjected to democratic regulation, cannot exist without a political–institutional environment that supports them and allows for their existence. The many examples of social or solidarity economies documented by such authors as Ash Amin (2009) and J. K. Gibson-Graham (2006) all highlight that such experiments cannot survive outside a supportive political environment. This is also the lesson that can be drawn from Quebec, where social economies have expanded the most. Margaret Mendell, reporting on the experiences from Quebec, thus writes:

> We have learned in Quebec that an enabling environment that is not limited to accessing existing public policy tools and resources is essential for the social economy. Policy innovation for the social economy requires new *processes* of policy formation and *institutional innovation*. This means designing *intermediary inter-sectoral dialogue spaces* that represent the numerous actors involved in the social economy and those that share its objectives. Social economy actors must be and are the co-authors of numerous policies that have emerged in the last decade in Quebec. The development of this political capacity is critical. (Mendell, in Amin, 2009: 182)

In other words, economic democratization depends on political will. Economic experiments, while interesting and important for all those involved and affected, are circumscribed by the political environment into which they are embedded. It is precisely the decoupling of the economy from society and politics that causes its excesses in the first place—and insight that goes back to the work of such classics as Karl Polanyi (1977).

Brazilian economist Celso Furtado's explains in his book *In Search of a New Model* ("Em Busca de Novo Modelo," 2002), "Development policies have to be formulated based upon an explanation of the substantive ends we seek to achieve and not based upon the logic of the means set forth by the accumulation process controlled by transnational enterprises" (Furtado, 2002: 36, my translation). Furtado thus places himself with all those who have long critiqued the working of different markets, demonstrating their tendencies to undermine themselves, to erode social trust and sociability, to produce increasing inequalities, concentration of power, and to destroy the environment.

We need to urgently rethink what kinds of markets we want and need and devise ways on how to keep markets competitive and accessible to the majority—every generation anew. The group we need to focus on the most are not the poor, but the rich and the superrich, as it is because of them that our markets are distorted and exclusive. They are also the ones who are responsible for diminishing the amount of goods available to the majority. Instead of focusing our attention on "welfare" and assistance policies for the poor, we need to spend much more energy thinking about curbing the assets, earnings, and political influence of the rich.

Upper limits to how much wealth a single person or family can hold, coupled with upper limits to income will make goods, or goods sold at luxury prices, unattainable. The most likely consequence is that the prices of such goods will drop to a point where the available supply meets demand. If upper limits to wealth and income are combined with severe restrictions on intergenerational inheritance, then this package of policies will reinvigorate markets tremendously by reintroducing all those goods hitherto reserved for 1 percent of the population. Instead of economic growth, we would enter a phase of economic recycling, which, considering our looming ecological disaster, seems all too necessary.

Such invigorated markets will be fair, particularly if coupled with policies of reparations and start-up funds.

Competition will still exist, together with all the incentives to succeed and excel—but it will be a much fairer competition as all will have a fair chance to win at one time or another. And it will be a competition within limits established by every society and community. Excess will be avoided, as a given community might decide to limit the number of cars or houses a single person or family can own, or how much land one person or family can hold.

Such upper limits to asset holdings will also have the "side-effect" of slowing down economic expansion and growth and eventually even bring it to a halt. This is so because, with upper limits to asset holding and severe limits to inheritance in place, tradeable goods will return to general markets in the next generation, thus forming the foundations of a sustainable, zero-growth economy, based on economic recycling.

EUROPEAN UNION

The only legitimate lawmaking is the one that occurs "bottom-up," with broad citizen participation. Laws made by organizations and institutions far removed from the realities they affect and regulate are illegitimate. This is another lesson that the progressive left did not learn from the Brexit case, as well as similar and related scenarios, when average citizens voted against EU membership or an EU constitution, drafted by a group of unknown "wise men" whom most EU citizens did not elect and did not know. Most people, I think it is safe to say, value the benefits the EU has brought: unrestricted border crossing, one currency in the whole region, and an overcoming of very old divisions and animosities, thus making Europe less prone to intra-European conflict and war. Particularly the younger generations see themselves more and more as "Europeans" and spend time in one of the EU countries, be it as part of their studies, in their vacations, or for work. At the same time, politicians and their programs seem unwilling or unable to see what many EU citizens, myself included, find problematic about the EU: a group of people, elected by very few and known by even less, sitting in Brussels or Strasbourg, passing laws that affect and regulate our daily lives and making decisions that affect all of us.

Clearly, what is needed is a more differentiated debate about the EU, beyond staying in it or leaving it. From the perspective advocated in this book a profound rethinking of the European Parliament, the European Commission, and the European Council, the three institutions responsible for EU lawmaking, is necessary. Particularly the European Parliament should be rethought as the 751 representatives currently serving in the European parliament together represent some 512 million EU citizens, so that each member represents 618,758 people. It is very difficult to imagine what kind of representation this can possibly be. The principle of subsidiarity, anchored in the Treaty on the European Union and the EU Protocol, already demands that political and legal decisions should preferably be taken by the member states and that EU institutions should only get involved when such decisions cannot sufficiently be achieved by the member states.

Lawmaking, as I have argued, should be a local affair and involve all those affected, if possible. If that is not possible, then sortition is a much more democratic way of selecting representatives of the population. The same logic applies to the EU institutions. To democratize the EU, its institutions need to be stripped of their (political) elitism and elected representatives replaced with average EU citizens, selected through stratified sortition to ensure that different groups are represented in Brussels, Strasbourg, and Luxembourg.

This is different from stating that the EU should end. We need to find ways how to keep and deepen the benefits the EU has brought to its member states and their citizens, namely, free border crossing, a single currency, and a climate of intra-European understanding and respect—while ending those that have, for good reason, angered many and brought some member states to vote for leaving the EU.

Substituting the European Parliament with a European Deliberative Body of randomly selected EU citizens might offer a possible solution to the current democratic deficit of the EU. However, most research on true or direct democracy insists that democracy can only be effectively practiced in small groups (Gastil, 2014) and it remains questionable if laws made at the supranational level can ever be legitimate. Ideally, lawmaking should be as local an affair as possible.

CORPORATIONS RETHOUGHT

Collectively owned businesses are not a bad thing. Publicly traded businesses are not a bad thing per se either. The rage and at times outrage directed against corporations, in my assessment, is not based on the form itself, but instead against how powerful some corporations have become and how reckless and influential in their narrow pursuit of profit. Avoiding the kind of undue political influence many powerful corporations currently exercise demands that campaign contributions and lobbying must be severely restricted and probably all together prohibited. The fact that some corporations have grown so big and powerful that they can influence whole countries, cities, and regions simply by threatening to leave or by not paying taxes in specific locations indicates that upper limits must also be applied to legal persons, not just physical ones.

Corporations were first created to facilitate public works and large infrastructure projects that demanded more investment than a single company, or even the government, could afford (Roy, 1999). We, as a collective, should decide if we want and need corporations, how many of them, and how large and powerful we want them to grow. There is no benefit whatsoever in letting corporations get away with polluting our environment for the sake of profit; with influencing our lawmakers so they lower corporate taxes; or with withholding taxes from those localities where profits are made. The kind of reinvigorated democratic governance I am prosing in this book also demands democratic control over markets and hence corporations.

Possible reforms could include the undoing of limited liability laws currently protecting corporate boards and managers. For corporations to truly serve as publicly owned entities, average shareholders should also be able to gain greater influence and control over corporate management. The overarching principle that must guide our attitudes and actions to corporations is the same that has guided the other proposals advanced in this book: democratic control and rule by average people, citizens, and shareholders (in this case), directed against the elite control exercised by politicians, managers, boards of directors, or CEOs.

While it can be argued that we need large corporations so that we can take on large tasks, benefitting large groups of people that require more money than any single, private company can raise, the stock market has very questionable benefits and has led to very large distortions. Today, operating under old paradigms, most people buy stock not because they want to actively be involved in a company as stock- and stakeholders—but because they hope to make a lot of money, without having to work for it.

Others know that they need to supplement their retirement income, given the precariousness of most retirement schemes in most countries of this world. Both of these motivations are not directly related to public ownership of large companies. If securing our retirements were a priority, as it should be, less people would feel the need to invest to secure their future. If free health care for all would be a guarantee, as it should be, then average people would not need to speculate on the stock market. The other motivation, of earning large amounts of money without working for it, comes close to playing the lottery—and it is also nurtured by the extreme inequalities we are all exposed to today. We see and read about the glamorous lives of the rich every day, thus instilling, in all of us, the wish to also own a yacht, to also spend vacations in Bora Bora, and to also own an Italian sports car.

Owning shares of a publicly traded company must come with the responsibility to actually participate in the governance of this company—not just a way of betting on the stock market. If that were the case, stock ownership would be radically reduced to those who actually have an interest in corporate business and publicly traded companies would come closer to the model of cooperatives.

FREE TRADE

Of all the markets we have and need, the financial market is certainly the one that requires the most regulation. Free trade, in itself, is a positive arrangement that has the potential to benefit all who participate—under certain conditions and as long as certain rules are followed. However, free trade so far has been anything but free. Instead, powerful nations, like the United States, but also many European countries, have forced open borders onto small nations while protecting their own productions with tariffs. Free trade is part of the human freedom to barter and engage with others in material exchanges and as such must be protected. However, capitalist markets tend to undermine trust and sociability, particularly when market interactions are virtual and long distance. Local markets and marketplaces, to the contrary, can build trust and sociability—particularly when trade is done repeatedly. We thus need to find ways to bolster and support local markets and hence local production and to restrict international trade. International trade poses a great onus on the environment, bringing with it risks of oil spills and pollution. Instead of outlawing international trade, we should device ways that protect local markets, thus making it more lucrative, within the upper limits established by a community, to trade locally than internationally. As the Corona virus crisis makes all too evident, relying too heavily on foreign trade creates extreme vulnerability while undermining local business. Instead of an "American first" policy we currently witness, we should advocate for a "local first" policy in support of local small businesses, particularly, but not only, in the area of food production.

FINANCIAL MARKETS

Upper limits need to put a break on how much money your money can earn you. One million dollars, at a 5 percent annual return, will earn you US $50,000 in interest alone—in the first year. If you do not spend that money but keep investing it, you will earn significantly more every year—$2,500 more in the first year and $13,814 more in the fifth year, as by then, you will have accumulated a total of US $1,276,281, which will earn you a total of US $63,814 in interest—if keeping at a, very conservative, 5 percent average annual return. In 2017, the average salary of a CEO working for one of the S&P 500 index companies was US $13.94 million per year. So instead of having your money earn you US $50,000 per year, the reality for many multimillionaires is that their money earns them US $500,000 in the first year. If instead of 10 million you had 1 billion to invest, your money will earn you $50 million in the first year. The world now has over 2,000 billionaires.

Earning such large amount of money without doing any work is not justifiable and not fair. It distorts all of our value systems and it leads to such a massive hording of opportunities for the offspring of multimillionaires and billionaires that it is next to impossible to win any competition against them. Earnings on investments need to be limited.

JUSTICE, FAIRNESS, AND EQUAL OPPORTUNITIES ACHIEVED?

Justice and fairness will most likely never be fully achieved. But we should nevertheless constantly strive to achieve it as much as possible. To get there, we need the right background political institutions. Right now, in most places of the world, the already privileged receive better education, better health care, have better job opportunities, pay less taxes, and control politics more than average people. They then seek to entrench their privileges and pass them on to their children. This is normal, rational behavior. As a society, however, we should find ways to support the neediest, not the already privileged, and counterbalance the unfair advantages of some over others. That is the mandate of justice, fairness, and equal opportunity.

This requires active political engagement. Fairness and equal opportunity will not come about by themselves—and they will not be delivered to us by others. The proposals advanced in this book outline some of the necessary background institutions able to protect justice, fairness, and equal opportunity—but democratic societies need to be constantly on the lookout for people and groups who constantly seek new ways of building up privilege and passing it on to the next generation. Democratic societies should be wary of the rich and powerful at all times, as they are the natural enemies of democracy, understood as the rule by average people.

OTHER MEASURES TO LIMIT OUR ECOLOGICAL FOOTPRINT AND CURB GLOBAL WARMING

As I write these lines, the world is on lockdown due to the Corona Virus, COVID-19. Without wanting to deny the seriousness and threat this pandemic poses to the world's population, particularly the most vulnerable among us, it is still worth considering the lessons we can draw from this experience. Venetians report cleaner water than ever in their canals, spotting fish they had not seen in decades. New York reports a 5 to 10 percent drop in CO_2 emissions. In Tampa,

Florida, where I write these lines, cruise ships have stopped operating, allowing marine life to recover. Concrete numbers are not available for many cities and places, but it is clear that the economic slowdown this crisis has brought offers a short respire for our strained environments.

As many universities and companies are shifting to home office regimes and online delivery of goods and services, the world is building up capacities to continue functioning while staying at home. These capacities could and should be used to provide nature with planned recovery days. Examples already exist. In Bogotá, the capital of Colombia, and in Mexico City, highways are blocked off on Sundays. In Bogotá, on average, a quarter of the population, some 1.7 million Bogotanos, use these car free zones in the middle of the city every Sunday for strolls and to ride their bikes. Car-free Sundays provide cities with space for leisure and exercise—and they allow the environment to recover, even if only for a limited amount of time. Corona has shown us that such car-free Sundays are well within the possible, particularly if public transportation is available.

Working from home for a day of the week also seems a possibility for many employees, as Corona is showing us. Instituting a day of the week as "home office day" would have a significant impact on the environment—reducing traffic and providing a temporary relief of CO_2 emissions by bringing average CO_2 emission down. Nature needs such regular breaks from economic activity.

COVID-19 has also shown us that our governments are able to provide financial help if they want to. The economic emergency packages passed during COVID-19 leave no doubt that our governments have the means to support their own citizens when they are in need. A whole set of arguments, routinely made by fiscal conservatives, was proven wrong during the COVID crisis. The lesson is clear: the money to finance start-up funds and reparations is available. Paying it is not a question of possibility, but of political will—and the only political will that should count in a democracy is the will of the people, particularly those affected by a policy. It is a great distortion of democracy when professional politicians decide about the fate of citizens in questions where they have nothing at stake.

I started this book by stating that crises provide opportunities, so it seems appropriate to end it on the same note: despite all the negative impacts the COVID-19 has brought us, it also increased our capacity to work from home thus bearing the potential to decrease our ecological footprint and it has shown us that only a few days without massive traffic already allows nature to recover. Imagine your city with major highways reserved for pedestrians and cyclists on Sundays. What a lovely Sunday it would be.

FINAL CONSIDERATIONS

There are, of course, many more implications and consequences, some of which unforeseen and non-intended, to establishing upper limits, enact legal duty, pay reparations to the historically disadvantaged, and enact laws to predistribute assets. Practice and experience will have to show them to us so we can face them and hopefully deal with them.

I am confident that we will be able to do just that while saving our planet and protecting fairness and equal opportunity for all. Fairness and equal opportunity will never lead to true equality—nor should they. Inequalities of outcomes are ok and acceptable, as long as they remain of no consequence for future generations. What should be unacceptable to all is that some people are born into privilege and never had to earn it or work for it.

If we gradually get rid of professional politicians, chances are that we get rid of a lot of war, extremism, hatred, and bigotry because politicians are more extreme than average citizens. They are the ones driving us into wars, pitching us against each other, and seeding hatred and division among us. They spread false accusations and exaggerate our differences.

Most people want peace, respect, opportunity, and fairness. Politicians hide some facts and exaggerate others—all so they can get voters behind them. As long as politics remains in the hands of the few who rule over others and take decisions for them, manipulation and abuse must remain a part of politics, as there is no reliable way to ensure that someone "represents" another truthfully and reliably. In the EU and in countries like India and the United States of America, where one elected politician represents hundreds of thousands of citizens, political alienation must inevitably follow.

The old ideology that people cannot rule themselves has lost all its legitimacy—if it ever had any as even an illiterate person knows better what is good for him or her than someone else. Politics does not require special knowledge. If it would, we would have a broad variety of specialists represented in the congresses and parliaments of the world. What we have instead is a majority of lawyers and former civil servants, joined by traditional economic elites. Nowhere does congress or parliament adequately represent the diversity of the people for and over whom they make decisions. Politics as a spectacle must end. We never had "philosopher kings" running our affairs—and we do not need them. We can run our own affairs.

Extreme voices are fanned and cultivated by the media, who tends to only report extreme and outrageous events and people, thus giving us the impression that our world is filled with lunatics and extremists. The media, in most countries, and even globally, owned by a few companies and families, have for too long spread fear and division among average people. Not only does the mainstream media focus exclusively on "bad news"—all of the most powerful media outlets are owned by elites themselves, who tend to support elitist politics and policies. If we consider the power of fake news and add it to the "normal" manipulation of opinion that average citizens are exposed to, we must find that the media has played a thoroughly negative role in our democracies. Democratizing democracy thus requires democratizing the media and not allowing, as a collective, some powerful moguls, "influencers," and hateful manipulators, to distort our knowledge of reality.

Extremism fares well among all those who lack practical knowledge. It is much easier to be a warmonger if you have never experienced war for yourself. By reducing and maybe one day eliminating the role of professional politicians and requiring that average citizens play a much larger role in politics, we can expect to push extremism back to where it belongs: at the extreme margins of society. In the meantime, applying the principle of stakeholdership to political leaders to ensure that they themselves are impacted by the decisions they make, promises to introduce morals and moderation back into politics. After all, it is much easier to decide over others, if you are not impacted by the decision yourself.

To get there, we need new paradigms that allow us to see our democratic and economic realities differently. Once we are able to push fairness and justice back into the center of our policies and actions, we can develop new institutions that rely much less on elites to run our public affairs and to regulate our markets. Elites and the rich are, after all, the enemies of true democracy, understood in its original sense as the rule of average people—and elites are also the ones undermining equal opportunities on markets. We need to shift our political attention away from the poor and focus on the rich instead if we want to address our current scenario of extreme inequality and environmental degradation.

Once we do so, by creating political institution that create and defend the political power and influence of all average people and block the influence of elites, we will not only create a vibrant political culture among all. By imposing upper limits to income and wealth, coupled with severe restrictions on inheritance, reparations and start-up funds for all those who cannot count on money from their families to become economic agents, we will not only protect politics and markets from elite abuse, but also the environment, as these measures will lead toward a truly sustainable economy, where tradeable goods return to general markets. Instead of relying on unsustainable growth and economic expansion, we will transition gradually to a zero-growth economy based on the principle of recycling, protective of the environment and securing our future survival on this planet.

NOTES

Preface

1 I treat fairness, as the equal opportunity to succeed compared to one's fellow citizens and I broadly follow Brian Barry's (2005) elaboration of social justice.
2 The Corona virus crisis has led to a severe loss of stock values in March 2020, the time I am writing these lines. While this is certainly true, it is also quite certain that the stock market will recover and compensate for the March 2020 losses, as the last severe stock market crisis of 2008 clearly showed. So while it might not appear that capital gains are as high as I claim in March 2020, they will again provide at least three times the return as work on the long run, which Piketty has captured in his famous formula: $r > g$, where r is the rate of return on capital and g is the rate of economic growth.

Chapter 3 Predistribution and Upper Limits

1 As already stated, my treatment of justice follows Brian Barry's (2005) elaboration of social justice.
2 The following sections of this chapter are taken from my book *The Crisis of Liberal Democracy and the Path Ahead*.
3 The document including Article 16 before its alterations can be accessed online at: http://founders.archives.gov/documents/Franklin/01-22-02-0314.
4 Document available online at: https://www.marxists.org/history/international/iwma/documents/1868/iasd-program.htm.

Chapter 4 Reparations

1 A preliminary version of this chapter was published in the journal *Kalfou* 6, no. 2 (December 2019): n/a.
2 According to *Measuring Worth*, £2 billion in 1945 currently amounts to:
   £77,800,000,000.00 using the retail price index;
   £71,400,000,000.00 using the GDP deflator;

£240,000,000,000.00 using the average earnings;
£294,000,000,000.00 using the per capita GDP; and
£390,000,000,000.00 using the share of GDP.

Measuring Worth, https://www.measuringworth.com/ppoweruk/, accessed 28 September 2019.

REFERENCES AND FURTHER READINGS

Abers, Rebecca. 2000. *Inventing Local Democracy*. Boulder, CO: Lynne Rienner.
Ackerman, Bruce, and Anne Alstott. 1999. *The Stake-Holder Society*. New Haven, CT: Yale University Press.
Agreement between the Government of the United States of America and the Government of the Federal Republic of Germany concerning the Foundation "Remembrance, Responsibility and the Future." July 17, 2000. https://1997–2001.state.gov/regions/eur/holocaust/000717_agreement.html. Last accessed September 28, 2019.
Aimer, P., and R. Miller. 2002. "Partisanship and Principle: Voters and the New Zealand Electoral Referendum of 1993." *European Journal of Political Research* 41, no. 6: 795–810.
Alba, Víctor. 2001. *Los Colectivizadores*. Barcelona: Laertes.
Albo, Greg, Sam Gindin, and Leo Panitch. 2010. *In and Out of Crisis*. Oakland, CA: PM Press.
Alcoff, Linda. 1991. "The Problem of Speaking for Others." *Cultural Critique*, Winter: 5–32.
Alexander, Michelle. 2012. *The New Jim Crow*. New York: New Press.
Alonso, Sonia, John Keane, and Wolfgang Merkel (eds.). 2011. *The Future of Representative Democracy*. Cambridge: Cambridge University Press.
Alperovitz, Gar, and Lew Daly. 2008. *Unjust Deserts*. New York: New Press.
Amin, Ash (ed.). 2009. *The Social Economy*. London: Zed Books.
Anderson, Benedict. 2006. *Imagined Communities*. New York: Verso.
Anderson, Carol. 2017. *White Rage: The Unspoken Truth of Our Racial Divide*. New York: Bloomsbury.
Anderson, Elizabeth. 2010. *The Imperative of Integration*. Princeton, NJ: Princeton University Press.
Arnold, Volker. 1985. *Rätebewegung und Rätetheorien in der Novemberrevolution*. Hamburg: JUNIUS Verlag.
Apter, David. 1968. "Notes for a Theory of Nondemocratic Representation." In *Nomos X*, chapter 19, pp. 278–317.
Arendt, Hannah. 1973. *The Origins of Totalitarianism*. New York: Harcourt, Brace, Jovanovich.
———. 1965. *On Revolution*. New York: Penguin.

Aristotle. 2009. *The Nicomachean Ethics*. Chicago, IL: University of Chicago Press.
———. 1892. *The Constitution of Athens*. Translated by E. Poste. London: MacMillan.
Arx, Nicolas von. 2002. *Aehnlich aber anders. Die Volksabstimmung in Kalifornien und in der Schweiz*. Basel: Helbing und Lichtenhahn.
Asante-Muhammed, Dedrick, Chuck Collins, Josh Hoxie, and Emanuel Nieves. 2016. "The Ever Growing Gap." Report, Institute for Policy Studies, Washington, DC. Available online: http://cfed.org/policy/federal/The_Ever_Growing_Gap-CFED_IPS-Final.pdf, last downloaded on August 10, 2016.
Atkinson, Anthony. 2015. *Inequality: What Can Be Done?* Cambridge, MA: Harvard University Press.
Auer, Andreas, and Michael Buetzer (eds.). 2001. *Direct Democracy: The Eastern and Central European Experience*. Aldershot: Ashgate.
Avritizer, Leonardo. 2009. *Participatory Institutions in Democratic Brazil*. Baltimore, MD: Johns Hopkins University Press.
Axelrod, Robert. 2006. *The Evolution of Cooperation*. New York: Basic Books.
Bahro, Rudolf. 1978. *The Alternative in Eastern Europe*. New York: Verso.
Balabkins, Nicholas. 1971. *West German Reparations to Israel*. New Brunswick, NJ: Rutgers University Press.
Baiocchi, Gianpaolo. 2005. *Militants and Citizens: The Politics of Participatory Democracy in Porto Alegre*. Stanford, CA: Stanford University Press.
Bakunin, Michail. 2011 [1873]. *Staatlichkeit und Anarchie*. Berlin: Karin Kramer Verlag.
———. 1977. *Sozial-politischer Briefwechsel*. Berlin: Karin Kramer Verlag.
Baratz, Dagania. 1945. *The Story of Palestine's First Collective Settlement*. Tel Aviv: Zionist Organization.
Barber, Benjamin. 1984. *Strong Democracy*. Los Angeles: University of California Press.
Baronnet, Bruno, Mariana Mora Bayo, and Richard Stahler-Sholk. 2011. *Luchas Muy Otras*. Mexico: UAM Press. Available online at: http://zapatismoyautonomia.wordpress.com.
Barry, Brian. 2005. *Why Social Justice Matters*. New York: Polity.
Bassok, Moti, and The Marker. 2009. "Israel to Seek Another 1b Euros Holocaust in Reparations from Germany." *Haaretz*, December 20. https://www.haaretz.com/1.4881652.
Bayle, Constantino. 1952. *Los Cabildos Seculares en la América Española*. Madrid: Sapientia, S.
Beitz, Charles. 1989. *Political Equality*. Princeton, NJ: Princeton University Press.
Bell, Derrick. 1974. "Dissection of a Dream." *Harvard Civil Rights—Civil Liberties Law Review* 9, no. 1: 165.
———. 1987. *And We Are Not Saved: The Elusive Quest for Racial Justice*. New York: Basic Books.
Benhabib, Seyla (ed.). 1996. *Democracy and Difference*. Princeton, NJ: Princeton University Press.
Berger, Peter, and Thomas Luckmann. 1966. *The Social Construction of Reality*. New York: Penguin Books.
Berlin, Isaiah. 1998. *The Proper Study of Mankind*. New York: Farrar, Strauss, and Giroux.
Beyer, Hans, and Ernst Engelberg. 1998 [1957]. *Von der Novemberrevolution zur Räterepublik in München*. Berlin: Herzog.
Bittker, Boris. 2003 [1973]. *The Case for Black Reparations*. Boston, MA: Beacon Press.
Blackmon, Douglas. 2009. *Slavery by Another Name*. New York: Anchor.

Blasi, Joseph Raphael. 1978. *The Communal Future: The Kibutz and the Utopian Dilemma.* Norwood, MA: Norwood Editions.
Bloch, Ernst. 1986. *The Principle of Hope.* New York: Blackwell.
Bookchin, Murray. 2015. *The Next Revolution.* New York: Verso.
———. 1996. *The Third Revolution*, vol. 1. London: Cassell.
——— 1998. *The Third Revolution*, vol. 2. London: Cassell.
———. 2004. *The Third Revolution*, vol. 3. London: Continuum.
———. 1994. *To Remember Spain.* San Francisco, CA: AK Press.
Bohman, John. 1998. "Survey Article: The Coming of Age of Deliberative Democracy." *Journal of Political Philosophy* 6, no. 4: 400–25.
Boix, Carles. 2015. *Political Order and Inequality.* New York: Cambridge.
Bonilla-Silva, Eduardo. 2013. *Racism without Racists.* Lanham, MD: Rowman & Littlefield.
Bowen, William, and Derek Bok. 2000. *The Shape of the River.* Princeton, NJ: Princeton University Press.
Bowler, Shaun, and Todd Donovan. 1998. *Demanding Choices: Opinion, Voting, and Direct Democracy.* Ann Arbor: University of Michigan Press.
———. 2002. "Democracy, Institutions, and Attitudes about Citizens Influence on Government." *British Journal of Political Science* 32: 371–90.
Bouchard, Merle (ed). 2013. *Innovation and the Social Economy: The Quebec Experience.* Toronto: University of Toronto Press.
Bourdieu, Pierre. 1984. *Distinction.* Cambridge, MA: Harvard University Press.
Bouricius, Terrill. 2013. "Democracy through Multi-Body Sortition: Athenian Lessons for the Modern Day." *Journal of Public Deliberation* 9, no. 1, Article 11.
Bowles, Samuel, and Herbert Gintis. 1998. "Recasting Egalitarianism." In *The Real Utopia Project*, edited by Eric Olin Wright. New York: Verso.
Brady, Henry, and David Collier. 2010. *Rethinking Social Inquiry.* New York: Rowman & Littlefield.
Bryan, Frank. 2003. *Real Democracy. The New England Town Meeting and How It Works.* Chicago, IL: University of Chicago Press.
Brooks, Roy (ed.). 1999. *When Sorry Isn't Enough.* New York: New York University Press.
Brown, Mark. 2006. "Survey Article: Citizen Panels and the Concept of Representation." *Journal of Political Philosophy*, 14: 203–25.
Budge, Ian. 1996. *The New Challenge of Direct Democracy.* Cambridge: Polity Press.
Bureau of European and Eurasian Affairs. 2006. "Report to Congress: German Foundation 'Remembrance, Responsibility, and the Future.'" March. U.S. Department of State, 2001–2009 Archive. http://2001-2009.state.gov/p/eur/rls/rpt/64401.htm.
Burke, Edmund. 1790 [1968]. *Reflections on the Revolution in France.* London: Penguin Books.
Buvinic, Mayra, Jaqueline Mazza, and Ruthanne Deutsch. 2004. *Social Inclusion and Economic Development in Latin America.* Washington/Baltimore: IDB/ Johns Hopkins University Press.
Callenbach, Ernest, and Michael Phillips. 2008. *A Citizen Legislature.* Exeter: Imprint Academic.
Carpenter, D. A. 1996. *The Reign of Henry III.* London: Hambledon Press.
Casanova, Julián. 2006. *Anarquismo y Revolución en la Sociedad Rural Aragonesa, 1936–1938.* Barcelona: Crítica.

Castoriadis, Cornelius. 2001. "The Retreat from Autonomy: Post-modernism as Generalised Conformism." *Democracy & Nature* 7, no. 1: 17–26.

———. 1990. "What Democracy?" In *Figures of the Unthinkable*. Open Manuscript.

———. 1985. "First Institution of Society and Second-Order Institutions." In *Figures of the Unthinkable*. Open Manuscript.

———. 1991. "Aeschylean Anthropogony and Sophoclean Self-Creation of Man." In *Figures of the Unthinkable*. Open Manuscript.

Chancel, Lucas, and Thomas Piketty. 2015. "Carbon and Inequality: From Kyoto to Paris." Paris School of Economics Working Paper, November 2015. Available online: http://piketty.pse.ens.fr/files/ChancelPiketty2015.pdf.

Christiano, Thomas. 1996. *The Rule of the Many*. Boulder, CO: Westview Press.

Christin, Thomas, Simon Hug, and Pascal Sciarini. 2002. "Interests and Information in Referendum Voting: An Analysis of Swiss Voters." *European Journal of Political Research* 41, no. 6: 759–76.

Claims Conference. 2014. "German Social Security Ghetto Pension—ZRBG." http://www.claimscon.org/what-we-do/compensation/germany-payments/zrbg/.

Clark, Susan, and Frank Bryan. 2005. *All Those in Favor: Rediscovering the Secrets of Town Meeting and Community*. Minneapolis, MN: Raven Mark.

Clarke, Harold, Allan Kornberg, and Marianne C. Stewart. 2004. "Referendum Voting as Political Choice: The Case of Quebec." *British Journal of Political Science* 34: 345–55.

Clayton, Joseph. 1908. *Robert Owen: Pioneer of Social Reforms*. London: A.C. Fifield.

Clastres, Pierre. 1989. *Society against the State*. New York: Zone Books.

Coates, Ta-Nehisi. 2014. "The Case for Reparations." *The Atlantic* (June): 1–63.

Cohen, Jean, and Andrew Arato. 1994. *Civil Society and Political Theory*. Cambridge, MA: MIT Press.

Cohen, Joshua, and Joel Rogers. 1995. "Associations and Democracy." In *The Real Utopias Project*, vol. 1, edited by Erik Olin Wright. London: Verso.

Cohen, Joshua, and Charles Sabel. 1997. "Directly-Deliberative Polyarchy." *European Law Journal* 3, no. 4 (December): 313–42.

Collins, Chuck, and Josh Hoxie. 2015. *Billionaire Bonanza: The Forbes 400 and the Rest of Us*. Boston, MA: Institute for Policy Studies.

Constant, Benjamin. 2003. *Principles of Government Applicable to all Governments*. Indianapolis, IN: Liberty Fund.

Corlett, Angelo. 2010. *Heirs of Oppression*. Lanham, MD: Rowman & Littlefield.

Credit Suisse. 2015. *Global Wealth Report*. Available online at: https://publications.credit-suisse.com/tasks/render/file/?fileID=F2425415-DCA7-80B8-EAD989AF9341D47E. Last accessed August 1, 2016.

Crenshaw, Kimberlé. 1988. "Race, Reform, and Retrenchment: Transformation and Legitimation in Antidiscrimination Law." *Harvard Law Review* 101, no. 7: 1331–87.

Cronin, Thomas. 1989. *Direct Democracy: The Politics of Initiative, Referendum, and Recall*. Cambridge, MA: Cambridge University Press.

Dahl, Robert A. 1989. *Democracy and Its Critics*. New Haven, CT: Yale University.

Dalby, Ben. 2002. "Slavery and the Question of Reparations." *International Socialist Review*, no. 20: 74–80.

Daly, Herman, and John Cobb. 1989. *For the Common Good*. Boston, MA: Beacon Press.

Darity, William, and Kirsten Mullen. 2020. *From Here to Equality: Reparations for Black Americans in the Twenty-First Century*. Durham: University of North Carolina Press.
Darity, William, and Samuel Myers. 1999. *Persistent Inequality: Race and Economic Inequality in the United States since 1945*. Northampton: Elgar.
Dawson, Michael. 2002. *Black Visions: The Roots of Contemporary African-American Political Ideologies*. Chicago, IL: University of Chicago Press.
Denver, D. 2002. "Voting in the 1997 Scottish and Welsh Devolution Referendums: Information, Interests, and Opinions." *European Journal of Political Research* 41, no. 6: 827–44.
Dettling, Lisa J., Joanne W. Hsu, Lindsay Jacobs, Kevin B. Moore, and Jeffrey P. Thompson. 2017. "Recent Trends in Wealth-Holding by Race and Ethnicity: Evidence from the Survey of Consumer Finances." FEDS Notes (September 27, 2017). Available online: https://www.federalreserve.gov/econres/notes/feds-notes/recent-trends-in-wealth-holding-by-race-and-ethnicity-evidence-from-the-survey-of-consumer-finances-20170927.htm. Last accessed September 28, 2019.
Doherty, Brian. 2008. *Radicals for Capitalism*. New York: Public Affairs.
Dore, Ronald. 2000. *Stock Market Capitalism: Welfare Capitalism*. Oxford: Oxford University Press.
Dovi, Suzanne. 2007. *The Good Representative*. New York: Wiley-Blackwell Publishing.
Dowbor, Ladislau. 2012. *Economic Democracy*. Creative Commons: Ladislau Dowbor: http://dowbor.org.
Downs, Anthony. 1957. *An Economic Theory of Democracy*. New York: Harper.
Dryzek, John, and Simon Niemeyer. 2008. "Discursive Representation." *American Political Science Review* 102, no. 4: 481–93.
Dryzek, John. 1996. "Political Inclusion and the Dynamics of Democratization." *American Political Science Review*, 90 (September): 475–87.
Dubois, Laurent. 2005. *Avengers of the New World: The Story of the Haitian Revolution*. New York: Belknap.
———. 2004. *A Colony of Citizens: Revolution and Slave Emancipation in the French Caribbean*. Durham: University of North Carolina Press.
Duffy, Bella. 2011 [1892]. *The Tuscan Republics*. New York: G.P. Putnam.
Dunbar, R. I. 1992. "Neocortex Size as a Constraint on Group Size in Primates." *Journal of Human Evolution* 22, no. 6: 469–93.
Edgerton, William (ed.). 1993. *Memories of Peasant Tolstoyans in Soviet Russia*. Bloomington: Indiana University Press.
Edwards, Steward. 1971. *The Paris Commune, 1871*. New York: Quadrangle Books.
Ellis, Richard. 2002. *Democratic Delusions: The Initiative Process in America*. Lawrence: University of Kansas Press.
Elster, John. 1998. *Deliberative Democracy*. New York: Cambridge University Press.
Engert, Stephan. 2010. "A Case Study in 'Atonement': Adenauer's Holocaust Apology." *Israeli Journal of Foreign Affairs* 4, no. 3: 111–22.
Escobar, Arturo. 2018. *Designs for the Pluriverse*. Durham, NC: Duke University Press.
Enzensberger, Hans Magnus. 1977. *Der kurze Sommer der Anarchie*. Frankfurt: Suhrkamp.

Fagotto, Elena, and Archon Fung. 2006. "Empowered Participation in Urban Governance: The Minneapolis Neighborhood Revitalization Program." *International Journal of Urban and Regional Research* 30, no. 3 (September): 638–55.
Felber, Christian. 2010. *Die Gemeinwohl-Ökonomie.* Wien: Deuticke.
Feld, Lars, and Gebhard Kirchgaessner. 2001. "Does Direct Democracy Reduce Public Debt? Evidence from Swiss Municipalities." *Public Choice* 109: 347–70.
———. 2001a. "The Political Economy of Direct Legislation: Direct Democracy and Local Decision-Making." *Economic Policy* (October): 331–67.
Feld, Lars, and Marcel Savioz. 1997. "Direct Democracy Matters for Economic Performance: An Empirical Investigation." *Kyklos* 50: 507–67.
Fiorina, Morris. 1999. "Extreme Voices: The Dark Side of Civic Engagement." In *Civic Engagement in American Democracy*, edited by Theda Skocpol and Morris Fiorina, 395–425. Washington, DC: Brookings Institution Press.
Fishkin, John. 1995. *The Voice of the People: Public Opinion and Democracy.* New Haven, CT: Yale University Press.
Foner, Eric. 2014. *Reconstruction.* New York: Perennial Classics.
Forbes, Jack. 2008. *Columbus and Other Cannibals.* New York: Seven Stories Press.
Frank, Robert. 2011. *The Darwin Economy.* Princeton, NJ: Princeton University Press.
———. 1999. *Luxury Fever.* Princeton, NJ: Princeton University Press.
Freire, A., and M. A. Baum. 2003. "Referenda Voting in Portugal, 1998: The Effects of Party Sympathies, Social Structure, and Pressure Groups." *European Journal of Political Research* 42, no. 1: 135–61.
Fraser, Nancy. 1989. *Unruly Practices: Power, Discourse, and Gender in Contemporary Social Theory.* Minneapolis: University of Minnesota Press.
———. 1997. *Justice Interruptus.* New York: Routledge.
———. 1998. "Heterosexism, Misrecognition and Capitalism: A Response to Judith Butler." *New Left Review* 228 (March/April): 140–49.
Freitag, Markus, and Adrian Vatter. 2000. "Direkte Demokratie, Konkordanz und Wirtschaftsleistung: Ein Vergleich der Schweizer Kantone." *Schweiz. Zeitschrift fuer Volkswirtschaft und Statistik* 136, no. 4: 579–606.
Frey, Bruno, and Alois Stutzer. 2002. *Happiness and Economics: How the Economy and Institutions Affect Human Well-Being.* Princeton, NJ: Princeton University Press.
Fung, Archon. 2006. *Empowered Participation: Reinventing Urban Democracy.* Princeton, NJ: Princeton University Press.
Furtado, Celso. 2002. *Em busca de novo modelo. Reflexões sobe a crise contemporânea.* Rio de Janeiro: Paz e Terra.
Gallagher, Michael, and Pier Vincenzo Uleri (eds.). 1996. *The Referendum Experience in Europe.* London: MacMillan.
Garnett, R. G. 1972. *Co-operation and the Owenite Socialist Communities in Britain, 1825–45.* Manchester: Manchester University Press.
George, Henry. 2006 [1880]. *Progress and Poverty.* Edited and abridged by Bob Drake. New York: Robert Schalkenbach Foundation.
George, Alexander, and Andrew Bennett. 2005. *Case Studies and Theory Development in the Social Sciences.* Cambridge, MA: MIT Press.
Gerring, John. 2012. *Social Science Methodology.* New York: Cambridge University Press.

Gibson-Graham, J. K. 2006. *A Postcapitalist Politics*. Minneapolis: University of Minnesota Press.
———. 1996. *The End of Capitalism as We Knew It*. Minneapolis: University of Minnesota Press.
Gilens, Martin, and Benjamin Page. 2014. "Testing Theories of American Politics: Elites, Interest Groups, and Average Citizens." *Perspectives on Politics* 12, no. 3 (September): 564–81.
Gómez, Luis. 2003. *El Alto de pie*. Bolivia: Textos Rebeldes.
Gould, Roger. 1995. *Insurgent Identities: Class, Community and Protest in Paris from 1848 to the Commune*. Chicago, IL: University of Chicago Press.
Gruner, Erich, and Hanspeter Hertig. 1983. *Der Stimmbuerger und die "neue" Politik*. Bern: Haupt.
Guinier, Lani. 1994. *The Tyranny of the Majority: Fundamental Fairness in Representative Democracy*. New York: Free Press.
Gutmann, Amy, and Dennis Thompson. 2004. *Why Deliberative Democracy?* Princeton, NJ: Princeton University Press.
Habermann, Frederike. 2009. *Halbsinseln gegen den Strom*. Frankfurt: Helmer Verlag.
Habermas, Jürgen. 1998. *Between Facts and Norms*. Cambridge, MA: MIT Press.
———. 1995. *The Theory of Communicative Action*. New York: Beacon Press.
Hacker, Jacob. 2011. *The Institutional Foundation of Middle-Class Democracy*. London: Policy Network.
Haney-Lopez, Ian. 2006. *White by Law*. New York: New York University Press.
Hansen, Mogens Herman. 1999. *The Athenian Democracy in the Age of Demosthenes*. Nebraska: University of Oklahoma Press.
Hansen, Peo, and Stefan Jonson. 2014. *Eurafrica: The Untold History of European Integration and Colonialism*. New York. Bloomsbury.
Hardin, Russell. 2004. "Representing Ignorance." *Social Philosophy and Policy*, 21: 76–99.
Hardt, Michael, and Antonio Negri. 2001. *Empire*. Cambridge, MA: Harvard University Press.
Harrington, James. 1656. *The Commonwealth of Oceana*. Manuscript available online at: http://www.gutenberg.org/ebooks/2801.
Harris, Cheryl. 1993. "Whiteness as Property." *Harvard Law Review* 106, no. 8: 1710–91.
Harrison, John. 2009. *Robert Owen and the Owenites in Britain and America*. New York: Routledge.
Harvey, David. 2011. *The Enigma of Capital*. New York: Oxford University Press.
———. 2014. *Seventeen Contradictions and the End of Capitalism*. New York: Oxford University Press.
Harvey, Neil. 1998. *The Chiapas Rebellion*. Durham, NC: Duke University Press.
Hattersley, Roy. 1987. *Chose Freedom*. London: Michael Joseph.
Hayes, Peter. 2004. "Forced and Slave Labor: The State of the Field." In *Forced and Slave Labor in Nazi-Dominated Europe: Symposium Presentations*, 1–8. Washington, DC: United States Holocaust Memorial Museum.
Henderson, Hazel. 2011. "Real Economies and the Illusions of Abstraction." *CADMUS* 1, no. 3 (October): 60–65.
Held, David. 1987. *Models of Democracy*. Cambridge, MA: Polity Press.
Helg, Aline. 1995. *Our Rightful Share: The Afro-Cuban Struggle for Equality, 1886–1912*. Chapel Hill: University of North Carolina Press.

Hero, Rodney, and Caroline Tolbert. 2004. "Minority Voices and Citizen Attitudes about Government Responsiveness in the American States: Do Social and Institutional Context Matter?" *British Journal of Political Science* 34: 109–21.
Higley, John, and Ian McAllister. 2002. "Elite Division and Voter Confusion: Australia's Republic Referendum in 1999." *European Journal for Political Research* 41, no. 6: 845–63.
Hiller, Helmut, and Stephan Füssel. 2006. *Wörterbuch des Buches*. Frankfurt/Main: V. Klostermann.
Hirsch, Fred. 1976. *Social Limits to Growth*. Cambridge, MA: Harvard University Press.
Hostetler, John. 1993. *Amish Society*. Baltimore, MD: Johns Hopkins University Press.
Hostetler, John, and Gertrude Enders Huntington. 1996. *The Hutterites in North America*. Stanford, CA: Stanford University Press.
Holloway, John. 2010. *Change the World without Taking Power*. London: Pluto Press.
Holt, Thomas. 1991. *The Problem of Freedom: Race, Labor, and Politics in Jamaica and Britain, 1832–1938*. Baltimore, MD: Johns Hopkins University Press.
Hooker, Juliet. 2009. *Race and the Politics of Solidarity*. New York: Oxford University Press.
Hug, Simon. 2002. *Voices of Europe: Citizens, Referendums, and European Integration*. Lanham, MD: Rowman & Littlefield.
Hug, Simon, and Pascal Sciarini. 2000. "Referendums on European Integration: Do Institutions Matter in the Voter's Decision?" *Comparative Political Studies* 33: 3–36.
Huntington, Samuel. 1991. *The Third Wave*. Nebraska: University of Oklahoma Press.
Jackson, Tim. 2009. *Prosperity without Growth*. Abington and New York: Earthscan.
Jaspers, Karl. 1946. *Die Schuldfrage. Ein Beitrag zur deutschen Frage*. Zürich: Artemis.
Katznelson, Ira. 2005. *When Affirmative Action Was White*. New York: Norton and Norton.
Kaufman, Alexander (ed.). 2006. *Capabilities Equality*. New York: Routledge.
Kinkade, Athleen. 1973. *A Walden Two Experiment*. New York: William Morrow.
Kirchgaessner, Gebhard, Lars Feld, and Marcel Savioz. 1999. *Die direkte Demokratie: Modern, erfolgreich, entwicklungs und exportfaehig*. Basel: Helbing und Lichtenhahn.
Klein, Naomi. 2014. *This Changes Everything: Capitalism vs. the Climate*. New York: Simon & Schuster.
——— 2008. *The Shock Doctrine: The Rise of Disaster Capitalism*. New York: Picador.
Knoll, Andalusia, and Silvia Rivera Cusicanqui. 2007. "Anarchism and Indigenous Resistance in Bolivia: Interview with Silvia Rivera Cusiqanqui." *World War 4 Report*, 1 October. Available online at: http://ww4report.com/node/4501. Last accessed February 22, 2015.
Kobach, Kris. 1993. *The Referendum: Direct Democracy in Switzerland*. Aldershot: Dartmouth University Press.
Kraybill, Donald. 2001. *The Riddle of Amish Culture*. Baltimore, MD: Johns Hopkins University Press.
Kretzmann, J. and J. McKnight. 1993. *Building Communities from the Inside Out*. Evanston, IL: ABCD Institute, Northwestern University.
Kriesi, Hanspeter. 2008. *Direct Democratic Choice: The Swiss Experience*. Lanham, MD: Lexington Books.
Kropotkin, Peter Harry. [1902] 2014. *Mutual Aid: A Factor of Evolution*. Seattle, WA: CreateSpace.
Kuhn, Gabriel (ed). 2012. *All Power to the Councils*. Oakland, CA: PM Press.

Kuhn, Thomas. 1996. *The Structure of Scientific Revolutions*. Chicago, IL: University of Chicago Press.
Lavy, George. 1996. *Germany and Israel*. London: Frank Cass.
Laclau, Ernesto, and Chantal Mouffe. 1985. *Hegemony and Socialist Strategy*. New York: Verso.
Laloux, Frederic. 2014. *Reinventing Organizations*. Millis, MA: Nelson Parker.
Lascher, Edward, Michael Hagen, and Steven Rochlin. 1996. "Gun behind the Door? Ballor Initiatives, State Policies and Public Opinion." *Journal of Politics* 58, no. 3: 760–75.
Layard, Richard. 2005. *Happiness*. New York: Penguin.
Le Glay, Marcel. 2009. *A History of Rome*. West Sussex: Blackwell.
Leach, E. R. 1964. *Political Systems of Highland Burma*. London: C. Bell.
Lee, Dorothy. 1987. *Freedom and Culture*. Long Grove, IL: Waveland Press.
Lessig, Lawrence. 2019. *They Don't Represent US: Reclaiming Our Democracy*. New York: Dey Street Books.
Leveque, Pierre, and Pierre Vidal-Naquet. 1996. *Cleisthenes the Athenian*. New York: Humanity Books.
Levin, Henry, C. R. Belfield, P. Muening, and C. E. Rouse. (2007). *The Costs and Benefits of an Excellent Education for America's Children—Overview*. Teachers College, Columbia University.
Levitas, Ruth. 2013. *Utopia as Method*. New York: Palgrave MacMillan.
Linder, Wolf. 1994. *Swiss Democracy: Possible Solutions to Conflict in Multicultural Societies*. New York: St. Martin's Press.
Lipsitz, George. 1998. *The Possessive Investment in Whiteness*. Philadelphia, PA: Temple University Press.
Little, Daniel. 1998. *Microfoundations, Method, and Causation*. New Brunswick, NJ: Transaction Publishers.
Lorenzo Pellegrini, Lorenzo, and Luca Tasciotti. 2014. "Bhutan: Between Happiness and Horror." *Capitalism Nature Socialism* 25, no. 3: 103–9.
Loury, Glenn. 2002. *The Anatomy of Racial Inequality*. Cambridge, MA: Harvard University Press.
Lublin, David. 1999. *The Paradox of Representation: Racial Gerrymandering and Minority Interests in Congress*. Princeton, NJ: Princeton University Press.
Lucas, Erhard. 1974. *Märzrevolution 1920. Band 1*. Frankfurt: Verlag Roter Stern.
———. 1970. *Märzrevolution 1920. Der bewaffnete Arbeiteraufstand im Ruhrgebiet*. Frankfurt: Verlag Roter Stern.
Madison, James, Alexander Hamilton, and John Jay. 1787–8 [1987]. In *The Federalist Papers*, edited by Isaac Kramnick. Harmondsworth: Penguin.
Magleby, David.1984. *Direct Legislation: Voting on Ballot Propositions in the United States*. Baltimore, MD: Johns Hopkins University Press.
Mahoney, James, and Dietrich Rueschemeyer (eds.). 2003. *Comparative Historical Analysis in the Social Sciences*. New York: Cambridge University Press.
Mamani, Pablo. 2006. "Territory and Structures of Collective Action: Neighborhood Micro-Governments." *Ephemera* 6, no. 3: 276–86.
Mamdani, Mahmood. 1996. *Citizen and Subject*. Princeton, NJ: Princeton University Press.
Manin, Bernard. 1997. *The Principles of Representative Government*. Cambridge, MA: Cambridge University Press.

Manin, Bernard. 1987. "On Legitimacy and Political Deliberation." *Political Theory* no. 15 (August): 338–68.
Mansbridge, Jane. 2009. "A Selection Model of Representation." *Journal of Political Philosophy* 17, no. 4: 369–98.
———. 2004. "Representation Revisited: Introduction to the Case Against Electoral Accountability." *Democracy and Society* 2, no. 1): 12–13.
———. 2003. "Rethinking Representation." *American Political Science Review* 97, no. 4: 515–28.
———. 1980. *Beyond Adversary Democracy*. Chicago, IL: Chicago University Press.
Marx, Anthony. 1998. *Making Race and Nation*. New York: Cambridge University Press.
Marx, Karl. 2000 [1865]. *Value, Price, and Profit*. Amsterdam and New York: JAI/Elsevier Science.
Matsusaka, John. 2004. *For the Many of the Few: The Initiative, Public Policy, and American Democracy*. Chicago, IL: University of Chicago Press.
Mauss, Marcel. 2000. *The Gift*. New York: Norton & Norton.
Mazzocco, Philip, Timothy Brock, Gregory Brock, Kristina Olson, and Mahzatrin Banaji. 2006. "The Cost of Being Black." *DuBois Review* 3, no. 2: 261–97.
Meade, James E. 1965. *Efficiency, Equality, and the Ownership of Property*. Cambridge, MA: Harvard University Press.
Melman, Seymour. 2001. *After Capitalism*. New York: Knopf.
Mendelsohn, Matthew, and Fred Cutler. 2000. "The Effects of Referendums on Democratic Citizens: Information, Politization, Efficacy, and Tolerance." *British Journal of Political Science* 30, no. 4: 685–97.
Merriman, John. 2014. *Massacre: The Life and Death of the Paris Commune*. New York: Basic Books.
Mezzdra, Sandro. 2007. "Living in Transition: Toward a Heterolingual Theory of the Multitude." Eipcp multilingual webjournal. http://eipcp.net/transversal/1107/mezzadra/en.
Milgram, Stanley. 2009 [1974]. *Obedience to Authority*. New York: Harper & Row.
Mill, John Stuart. 2004. *Considerations on Representative Government*. Whitefish, MT: Kessinger Publishing.
Millar, Fergus. 1998. *The Crowd in Rome in the Late Republic*. Ann Arbor: University of Michigan Press.
Miller, Fred. 1997. *Nature, Justice, and Rights in Aristotle's Politics*. Oxford: Clarendon.
Mills, Charles. 1997. *The Racial Contract*. Ithaca, NY: Cornell University Press.
Mintz, Frank. 2006. *Autogestión y Anarcosindicalismo en la España revolucionaria*. Madrid: Traficantes de Suenos.
Moeckli, Silvano. 1994. *Direkte Demokratie: Ein internationaler Vergleich*. Bern: Haupt.
Möbes, Nancy. 2007. *Die Preisbindung für Bücher im deutschen Sprachraum unter den Bedingungen des Europäischen Gemeinschaftsrechts*. Diplomarbeit. Hochschule für Technik, Wirtschaft und Kultur Leipzig (FH). Fachbereich Medien Studiengang Verlagsherstellung.
Moore, John Preston. 1954. *The Cabildo in Peru under the Habsburgs*. Durham, NC: Duke University Press.
Mouffe, Chantal. 2013. *Agonistics: Thinking the World Politically*. New York: Verso.

Muni, S. D. 2014. "Bhutan's Deferential Democracy." *Journal of Democracy* 25, no. 2 (April): 158–63.
Muñera, Alfonso. 2011. *Tiempos difíciles: La república del XIX; Una ciudadanía incompleta*. Cartagena: Plumas de Mompox.
National Vital Statistics System. 2017. *National Vital Statistics Reports* 68, no. 7. Available online: https://www.cdc.gov/nchs/data/nvsr/nvsr68/nvsr68_07-508.pdf. Last accessed September 28, 2019.
Nadeau, Richard, Pierre Martin, and Andre Blais. 1999. "Attitude toward Risk-Taking and Individual Choice in the Quebec Referendum on Sovereignty." *British Journal of Political Science* 29: 523–39.
Neblo, Michael, Kevin Esterling, and David Lazer. 2018. *Politics with the People: Building a Direct Representative Democracy*. New York: Cambridge University Press.
Nef, Jorge, and Bernd Reiter. 2009. *The Democratic Challenge. Democratization and De-Democratization in Global Perspective*. New York: Palgrave MacMillan.
Neidhart, Leonhard. 1970. *Plebiszit und pluralitaere Demokratie: Eine Analyse der Funktion des schweizerischen Gesetzesreferendums*. Bern: Francke.
Neiman, Susan. 2019. Learning from the Germans: Race and the Memory of Evil. New York: Farrar, Straus and Giroux.
Nelson, Eric. 2004. *The Greek Tradition in Republican Thought*. New York: Cambridge University Press.
Nylen, William, and Lawrence Dodd. 2003. *Participatory Democracy versus Elitist Democracy: Lessons from Brazil*. New York: Palgrave Macmillan.
Offer, Avner. 2006. *The Challenge of Affluence*. Oxford: Oxford University Press.
Ogletree, Charles. 2004. *All Deliberate Speed: Reflections on the First Half-Century of* Brown v. Board of Education. New York: Norton.
Oliver, Melvin, and Thomas Shapiro. 2006. *Black Wealth/White Wealth: A New Perspective on Racial Inequality*. New York: Routledge.
O'Leary, Kevin. 2006. *Saving Democracy*. Stanford, CA: Stanford University Press.
O'Neill, Martin, and Thad Williamson (eds.). 2014. *Property-Owning Democracy: Rawls and Beyond*. Malden, MA: Wiley Blackwell.
Ostrom, Elenor. 2015. *Governing the Commons*. New York: Canto Classics.
Oxfam. 2015. "Wealth: Having It All and Wanting More." *Oxfam Issue Briefing*. Available online at: www.oxfam.org.
Packer, George. 2020. "We Are Living in a Failed State." *The Atlantic*. June 2020.
Pagès, Pelai. 2013. *El sueno igualitario entre los campesinos de Huesca [1936–1938]*. Huesca: Sariñena.
Palgim, Michal and Shulamit Reinharz (eds.). 2014. *100 Years of Kibbutz Life*. New Brunswick, NJ: Transaction Publishers.
Pannekoek, Anton. 2003. *Workers' Councils*. Edinburgh: AK Press.
Papadopoulos, Yannis. 2001. "How Does Direct Democracy Matter? The Impact of Referendum Votes in Parkinson, John. 2001. Who Knows Best? The Creation of the Citizen-Initiated Referendum in New Zealand." *Government and Opposition* 36, no. 3: 403–21.
Pateman, Carole. 1970. *Participation and Democratic Theory*. Cambridge, MA: Cambridge University Press.

Pennock, J. Roland, and John Chapman (eds.). 1968. *Representation*. New York: Atherton Press.
Perraudin, Michael, and Juergen Zimmerer. 2010. *German Colonialism and National Identity*. New York: Routledge.
PEW Research Center. 2013. "Black Unemployment Rate Is Consistently Twice That of Whites." *PEW Research Center Fact Tank*, published on August 21, 2013. Available online: https://www.pewresearch.org/fact-tank/2013/08/21/through-good-times-and-bad-black-unemployment-is-consistently-double-that-of-whites/. Last accessed September 28, 2019.
Piketty, Thomas. 2014. *Capital in the Twenty-First Century*. Cambridge, MA: Harvard and Belknap. Online version, available at: http://resistir.info/livros/piketty_capital_in_the_21_century_2014.pdf.
Pitkin, Hanna Fenichel. 2004. "Representation and Democracy: Uneasy Alliance." *Scandinavian Political Studies* 27, no. 3: 335–42.
———. 1967. *The Concept of Representation*. Berkeley: University of California.
Plato. 348 BCE. *Laws*. Translated by Benjamin Jowett. Available online at: http://www.gutenberg.org/ebooks/1750.
Plato. 2005. *Protagoras and Meno*. New York: Penguin Classics.
Plotke, David. 1997. "Representation Is Democracy." *Constellations*, 4: 19–34.
———. "Politics and Policy-Making." *West European Politics* 24, no. 2: 35–58.
———. 1998. *Démocratie directe*. Paris: Economica.
Pocock, J. G. A. 1981. "Virtues, Rights, and Manners: A Model for Historians of Political Thought." *Political Theory* 9, no. 3 (August): 353–68.
———. 2007. "The Ideal of Citizenship since Classical Times." In *Theorizing Citizenship*, edited by Ronald Beiner, 29–52. Albany, NY: SUNY Press.
Polanyi, Karl. 1977. *Livelihood of Man*. New York: Academic Press.
Przworksi, Adam, Susan C. Stokes, and Bernard Manin (eds.). 1999. *Democracy, Accountability, and Representation*. Cambridge, MA: Cambridge University Press.
Przeworski, Adam, and Henry Teune 1982. *The Logic of Comparative Social Inquiry*. New York: Krieger.
Psacharopoulos, George. 2007. *The Costs of School Failure: A Feasibility Study*. European Network on Economics of Education (EENEE).
Rawls, John. 2001. *Justice as Fairness: A Restatement*. Cambridge, MA: Harvard Belknap Press.
———. 1999. *A Theory of Justice*. Cambridge, MA: Harvard Belknap Press.
Ragin, Charles. 2000. *Fuzzy Set Social Science*. Chicago, IL: University of Chicago Press.
———. 2008. *Redesigning Social Inquiry: Fuzzy Sets and Beyond*. Chicago, IL: University of Chicago Press.
———. 2008b. User's Guide to Fuzzy-Set/Qualitative Comparative Analysis. Document available online at www.fsqca.com.
———. 1987. *The Comparative Method*. Berkeley: University of California Press.
Reed, Adolph. 2000. "Class Notes: The Case against Reparations." *The Progressive* (December). www.progressive.org. Available online at: https://nonsite.org/editorial/the-case-against-reparations. Last accessed September 28, 2019.
Rehfeld, Andrew. 2005. *The Concept of Constituency: Political Representation, Democratic Legitimacy and Institutional Design*. Cambridge, MA: Cambridge University Press.

———. 2006. "Towards a General Theory of Political Representation." *Journal of Politics*, 68: 1–21.

———. 2005. *The Concept of Constituency: Political Representation, Democratic Legitimacy and Institutional Design*. New York: Cambridge University Press.

Reiter, Bernd. 2013. *The Dialectics of Citizenship: Exploring Privilege, Exclusion, and Racialization*. East Lansing: Michigan State University Press.

———. 2019. *The Crisis of Liberal Democracy and the Path Ahead: Alternatives to Political Representation and Capitalism*. London: Rowman & Littlefield.

———. 2018. *Constructing the Pluriverse*. Durham, NC: Duke University Press.

Reybrouck, David van. 2018. *Against Elections*. New York: Seven Stories.

Ricardo, David. 1817: *On the Principles of Political Economy and Taxation*. Available online at: https://www.marxists.org/reference/subject/economics/ricardo/tax/ch01.htm.

Richardson, Henry. 2002. "Representative Government." In *Democratic Autonomy*, 193–202. Oxford: Oxford University Press.

Robinson, Cedric. 2000. *Black Marxism: The Making of the Black Radical Tradition*. Chapel Hill: University of North Carolina Press.

Robinson, Randall. 2000. *The Debt: What America Owes to Blacks*. New York: Dutton.

Roithmayr, Daria. 2014. *Reproducing Racism: How Everyday Choices Lock In White Advantage*. New York: New York University Press.

———. 2010. "Racial Cartels." *Michigan Journal of Race & Law* 16, no. 1: 45–79.

Rosenstone, Steven, and John Hansen. 1993. *Mobilization, Participation, and Democracy in America*. New York: MacMillan.

Rosner, Menahem. 2000. "Future Trends of the Kibbutz: An Assessment of Recent Changes." University of Haifa. The Institute for Study and Research of the Kibbutz. Publication No. 83. Available online: http://research.haifa.ac.il/~kibbutz/pdf/trends.PDF.

Rothstein, Richard. 2017. *The Color of Law: A Forgotten History of How Our Government Segregated America*. New York: Liveright.

Rousseau, Jean Jacques. 2003 [1762]. *The Social Contract*. Translated by Judith Masters and Roger Masters. New York: St. Martin's Press.

Roy, William. 1999. *Socializing Capital*. Princeton, NJ: Princeton University Press.

Runciman, David. 2010. "Hobbes's Theory of Representation: Anti-democratic or Protodemocratic." In *Political Representation*, edited by Ian Shapiro, Susan C. Stokes, Elisabeth Jean Wood, and Alexander Kirshner. Cambridge, MA: Cambridge University Press.

———. 2007. "The Paradox of Political Representation." *Journal of Political Philosophy*, 15: 93–114.

Russell, Raymond, Robert Hanneman, and Shlomo Getz. 2000. "Processes of Deinsitutionalization and Reinstitutionalization among Israeli Kibbutzim, 1990–1998." Paper presented at the Annual Meeting of the American Sociological Association. Washington, DC, August 12–16, 2000. Available online at: http://research.haifa.ac.il/~kibbutz/pdf/rusty2000.PDF.

Ryden, David K. 1996. *Representation in Crisis: The Constitution, Interest Groups, and Political Parties*. Albany: State University of New York Press.

Ryerson, Ricard Alan. 1978. *The Revolution Is Now Begun: The Radical Committees of Philadelphia, 1765–1776*. Philadelphia: University of Pennsylvania Press.

Sabato, Larry, Bruce Larson, and Howard Ernst (eds.). 2001. *Dangerous Democracy? The Battle over Ballot Initiatives in America*. Lanham, MD: Rowman & Littlefield.
Sabl, Andrew. 2002. *Ruling Passions: Political Offices and Democratic Ethics*. Princeton, NJ: Princeton University Press.
Sandel, Michael. 1998. *Democracy's Discontent*. New York: Belknap.
Santos, Boaventura de Sousa 2014. *Epistemologies of the South: Justice against Epistemicide*. Boulder, CO: Paradigm Publishers.
Saward, Michael. 2009. "Authorisation and Authenticity: Representation and the Unelected." *Journal of Political Philosophy*, 17: 1–22.
———. 2008. "Representation and Democracy: Revisions and Possibilities." *Sociology Compass*, 2: 1000–13.
———. (ed.). 2000. *Democratic Innovation: Deliberation, Representation and Association*. London: Routledge.
Schattschneider, E. E. 1960. *The Semisovereign People*. New York: Holt, Rinehart, and Winston.
Schmitter, Philippe. 2000. "Representation." In *How to Democratize the European Union and Why Bother?*, 53–74. Lanham, MD: Rowman and Littlefield.
Schneider, Carsten, and Claudius Wagemann. 2012. *Set-Theoretic Approaches for the Social Sciences*. New York: Cambridge University Press.
Schneider, Dieter, and Rudolf Kuda. 1969. *Arbeiteraete in der Novemberrevolution: Ideen, Wirkungen, Dokumente*. Frankfurt: Suhrkamp.
Schuchter, Arnold. 1970. *Reparations: The Black Manifesto and Its Challenge to White America*. Philadelphia, PA: Lippincott.
Schumpeter, Joseph. 1976. *Capitalism, Socialism, and Democracy*. London: Allen and Unwin.
Schwartz, Nancy. 1988. *The Blue Guitar: Political Representation and Community*. Chicago, IL: University of Chicago Press.
Sciarini, Pascal. 1994. *Le systeme politique suisse face a la Communaute europeenne et au GATT: Le cas-test de la politique agricole*. Geneve: Georg.
Sciarini, Pascal, and Lionel Marquis. 2000. "Opinion pubique et politique exterieure." *Revue suisse de science politique* 6, no. 3: 71–83.
Scott, James. 2009. *The Art of Not Being Governed*. New Haven, CT: Yale University Press.
———. 2017. *Against Grain*. New Haven and London: Yale University Press.
Segev, Tom. 1991. *The Seventh Million*. New York: Holt.
Sen, Amartya. 1999. *Development as Freedom*. New York: Oxford University Press.
———. 2009. *The Idea of Justice*. Cambridge, MA: Harvard Belknap Press.
Service, Elman. 1975. *Origins of the State and Civilization*. New York: W.W. Norton.
Shapiro, Ian, Susan C. Stokes, Elisabeth Jean Wood, and Alexander S. Kirshner (eds.). 2009. *Political Representation*. Cambridge, MA: Cambridge University Press.
Shapiro, Thomas. 2005. *The Hidden Cost of Being African American: How Wealth Perpetuates Inequality*. New York: Oxford University Press.
Sharkey, Patrick. 2013. *Stuck in Place*. Chicago, IL: University of Chicago Press.
Shatz, Marshall (ed.). 1971. *The Essential Works of Anarchism*. New York: Bantam Books.
Simon, Herbert. 1990. *Reason in Human Affairs*. Stanford, CA: Stanford University Press.
Sinnott, Richard. 2002. "Cleavages, Parties, and Referendums: Relationship between Representative and Direct Democracy in the Republic of Ireland." *European Journal of Political Research* 41, no. 6: 811–26.

Sitkoff, Harvard. 1981. *The Struggle for Black Equality, 1954–1980*. New York: Hill and Wang.
Sitrin, Marina, and Dario Azzelini. 2014. *They Can't Represent Us*. New York: Verso.
Slyomovics, Susan. 2014. *How to Accept German Reparations*. Philadelphia: University of Pennsylvania Press.
Smale, Alison. 2015. "Former SS Member, on Trial in Germany, Says He Was 'Morally Complicit' at Auschwitz." *New York Times*, April 21.
Smith, Adam. 1976 [1776]. *The Wealth of Nations*. New York: Bantam Classics.
Smith, Mark. 2001. "The Contingent Effects of Balloit Initiatives and Candidate Races on Rutnout." *American Journal of Political Science* 45, no. 3: 700–6.
Smith, Mark, and Caroline Tobert. 2004. *Educated by Initiative: The Effects of Direct Democracy on Citizens and Political Organizations in the American States*. Ann Arbor: University of Michigan Press.
Snyder, Richard, and Gabriel Torres (eds.). 1998. *The Future of the Ejido in Rural Mexico*. San Diego: University of California Press.
Sommer, Jeffrey. 2015. *Race, Reality, and Realpolitik*. Lanham, MD: Lexington Books.
Spiro, Medford. 1063. *The Kibbutz: Venture in Utopia*. New York: Schocken Books.
Stahler-Sholk, Richard. 2015. "Resistencia, Identidad, y Autonomia: La Transformacion de espacios en las comunidades Zapatistas." *Revista Pueblos y Fronteiras* 10, no. 19 (Junio–Noviembre): 197–226.
———. 2014. "Mexico: Autonomy, Collective Identity, and the Zapatista Social Movement." In *Rethinking Latin American Social Movements*, edited by Richard Stahler-Sholk, Harry Vanden, and Marc Becker, 187–207. Lanham, MD: Rowman & Littlefield.
Stutzer, Alois, and Bruno Frey. 2000. "Staerkere Volksrechte—Zufriedendere Buerger: eine mikrooekonomische Untersuchung fuer die Schweiz." *Schweiz. Zeitschrift fuer Politikwissenschaft* 6, no. 3: 1–30.
Sue, Christina. 2013. *Land of the Cosmic Race: Race Mixture, Racism, and Blackness in Mexico*. New York: Oxford University Press.
Sutherland, Keith. 2008. *A People's Parliament*. Exeter: Imprint Academic.
Svensson, Palle. 2002. "Five Danish Referendums on the European Community and European Union: A Critical Assessment of the Franklin Thesis." *European Journal of Political Research* 41, no. 6: 733–50.
Strolovitch, Dara Z. 2007. *Affirmative Advocacy: Race, Class, and Gender in Interest Group Politics*. Chicago, IL: Chicago University Press.
Tapia, Francisco Javier. 1965. *Cabildo Abierto Colonial*. Madrid: Ediciones Cultura Hispánica.
TATORT. 2013. *Democratic Autonomy in North Kursistan*. Hamburg: New Compass Press.
Telles, Edward. 2014. *Pigmentocracies: Ethnicity, Race, and Color in Latin America*. Chapel Hill: University of North Carolina Press.
Termes, Josep. 2011. *Historia del Anarquismo en España (1870–1980)*. Barcelona: RBA.
Thame, Maziki. 2011. "Reading Violence and Post-colonial Decolonization through Fanon: The Case of Jamaica." *Journal of Pan African Studies* 4, no. 7: 75–93.
Thucydides. 1954. *History of the Peloponnesian War*. New York: Penguin Classics.
Tilly, Charles. 1998. *Durable Inequality*. Berkeley: University of California Press.
Tocqueville, Alexis de. [1835] 1988: *Democracy in America*. New York: Harper.
Toennies, Ferdinand. 1988. *Community and Society*. New York: Transaction Publishers.

Tolbert, Caroline, Ramona McNeal, and Daniel Smith. 2003. "Enhancing Civic Engagement: The Effect of Direct Democracy on Political Participation and Knowledge." *State Politics and Policy Quarterly* 3, no. 1: 23–41.
Torpey, John. 2017. *Making Whole What Has Been Smashed: On Reparations Politics*. New Brunswick, NJ: Rutgers University Press.
Torre, Alejandro R. Diez. 2009. *Trabajan para la Eternidad: Colectividades de trabajo y ayuda mutual durante la Guerre Civil en Aragón*. Madrid y Zaragoza: Malatesta.
Trail, J. S. 1975. "The Political Organization of Attica." *Hesperia Supplements* 14: i–iii+v–xi+xiii-xviii+1–135+139–169.
Trechsel, Alexander. 2000. *Feuerwerk Volksrechte: Die Volksabstimmung in den schweizerischen Kantonen 1970–1996*. Basel: Helbing und Lichthahn
Truman, David. 1951. *The Governmental Process*. New York: Knopf.
Tully, James. 2008. *Public Philosophy in a New Key*. New York: Cambridge University Press.
Tusa, Ann, and John Tusa. 2010. *The Nuremberg Trial*. New York: Skyhorse.
United States Census Bureau. 2010 Census Data. Available here: https://www.bjs.gov/content/pub/pdf/p10.pdf. Last accessed September 28, 2019.
Urbinati, Nadia. 2000. "Representation as Advocacy: A Study of Democratic Deliberation." *Political Theory*, 28: 258–786.
Urbinati, Nadia, and Mark Warren. 2008. "The Concept of Representation in Contemporary Democratic Theory." *Annual Review of Political Science*, 11: 387–412.
Urma, Karma, Sabina Alkire, Tshoki Zangmo, Karma Wangdi. 2012. *An Extensive Analysis of GNH Index*. Centre for Bhutan Studies. Online document.
Vatter, Adrian. 2002. *Kantonale Demokratien im Vergleich. Enstehungsgruende, Interaktionen und Wirkungen politischer Institutionen in den Schweizer Kantonen*. Opladen: Leske+Budrich.
Veblen, Thorstein. 2009. *The Theory of the Leisure Class*. New York: Oxford University Press.
Verba, Sidney, and Norman Nie. 1972. *Participation in America*. New York: Harper and Row.
Vieira, Monica, and David Runciman. 2008. *Representation*. Cambridge, MA: Polity Press.
Victor, Peter, and Gideon Rosenbluth. 2007. "Managing without Growth." *Ecological Economics*, 61: 492–504.
Von Plato, Alexander, Almuth Leh, and Christoph Thonfeld (eds.). 2010. *Hitler's Slaves*. New York: Berghahn.
Wallace-Wells, David. 2019. *The Uninhabitable Earth*. New York: Tim Duggan Books.
Wampler, Brian. 2007. *Participatory Budgeting in Brazil*. University Park: Pennsylvania State University Press.
Warren, Mark. 2008. "Citizen Representatives." In *Designing Deliberative Democracy: The British Columbia Citizens' Assembly*, edited by Mark Warren and Hilary Pearse, 50–69. Cambridge, MA: Cambridge University Press.
———. 2001. *Democracy and Association*. Princeton, NJ: Princeton University Press.
Warren, Mark, and Dario Castiglione. 2004. "The Transformation of Democratic Representation." *Democracy and Society* 2, no. I: 5, 20–22.
Weber, Max. 1968. *Economy and Society*. Berkeley: University of California Press.
Wiesel, Elie. 1997. *Ethik und Erinnerung*. Berlin: Ernst Reuther Verlag.
Wilkinson, Richard, and Kate Picket. 2010. *The Spirit Level*. New York: Bloomsbury Press.
Williams, Melissa. 2000. "The Uneasy Alliance of Group Representation and Deliberative Democracy." In *Citizenship in Diverse Societies*, edited by W. Kymlicka and Wayne Norman, 124–153. Oxford: Oxford University Press.

Williamson, Abby, and Archon Fung. 2004. "Public Deliberation: Where We Are and Where Can We Go?" *National Civic Review* (Winter): 3–15.

Wilson, William. 1967. *The Angel and the Serpent: The Story of New Harmony*. Bloomington: Indiana University Press.

Wolff, Edward. 2001. "Racial Wealth Disparities." *Public Policy Brief*, no. 66A. Available online: http://www.levyinstitute.org/pubs/hili66a.pdf. Last accessed September 28, 2019.

Wolff, Edward N. 2014. *Household Wealth Trends in the United States, 1962–2013: What Happened Over the Great Recession?* Cambridge, MA: National Bureau of Economic Research.

Wright, Eric Olin. 2010. *Envisioning Real Utopias*. New York: Verso.

Wolff, Richard. 2012. *Democracy at Work*. Chicago: Haymarket Books.

World Bank. 2014. *Bhutan Development Update: April 2014*. Online document, available at: http://documents.worldbank.org/curated/en/2014/04/19455214/bhutan-development-update.

Young, Iris Marion. 1999. "Justice, Inclusion, and Deliberative Democracy." In *Deliberative Politics*, edited by Stephen Macedo. Oxford: Oxford University.

———. 1996. *Justice and the Politics of Difference*. Princeton, NJ: Princeton University Press.

———. 2000. *Inclusion and Democracy*. New York: Oxford University Press.

Yunus, Mohammed. 2003. *Banker to the Poor*. New York: Public Affairs.

Yurnbull, Colin. 1968. *The Forest People*. New York: Touchstone.

Zablocki, Benjamin. 1980. *Alienation and Charisma: A Study of Contemporary American Communes*. New York: Free Press.

Zaller, John. 1992. *The Nature and Origins of Mass Opinion*. Cambridge, MA: Cambridge University Press.

Zenker, E. V. 1984. *Der Anarchismus*. Berlin: Rixdorfer Verlagsanstalt.

Ziai, Aram. 2018. "Internationalism and Speaking for Others: What Struggling against Neoliberal Globalization Taught Me about Epistemology." In *Constructing the Pluriverse*, edited by Bernd Reiter, 117–36. Durham, NC: Duke University Press.

INDEX

Adams, John 21, 61–63
Amish 27
anarchism 22, 24–25, 64–65
Aristotle 58–61
Athens (classical) 6, 9, 28, 32, 59, 68
Atkinson, Anthony xvii, 53, 68

Bakunin, Mikhail 64–65
billionaires xii, 2, 10, 69, 100, 106–7
Black Panthers 84–85
Bolivia 26, 69, 95
Botswana 26
bureaucracy 23

Canada 32, 41, 49, 77, 96
capital, symbolic 100
Colombia 26, 77, 87, 91, 108
coloniality 76
commons xvii, 64
confederation 24, 31, 41
COVID-19 xii, 2, 107–108

degrowth 47, 56, 71
Denmark 51, 96
development 10, 14, 26, 36, 65, 67, 101–2
discipline xi, xv, 5

exclusion 11–12, 28, 40, 54, 74, 77
EU 8, 35, 103–4
European Parliament 103–4

fake news 6, 8, 43, 98–99, 110
federalism 31, 41, 43, 96

Fishkin, James xvi, 33, 35, 39, 41, 97
Fourier, Charles 64

George, Henry 63–64
German Räte Republic (1918) 23
growth xiii, xvi, 3, 11, 13–14, 19, 47, 53, 56, 71, 81, 95, 100, 102–3, 111

Habermas, Jürgen 27
Hacker, Jacob xvi–xvii, 67–68
Harvard xii, xvi, 3, 12, 46
health care 49, 52, 54–56, 68, 90, 95, 105, 107
House of Representatives xvii, 3, 34, 43
housing ix, x, 56, 74, 79, 84–85, 89–90
Hunter and Gatherers 9
Hutterites 27

Iceland 41–42
indigenous people xv, xvii–xviii, 9, 22, 26, 31–32, 47, 56–57, 64, 73–74, 76
Internet 16
Ireland 32, 41, 51

Jefferson, Thomas 61–64

kgotla 26
Kropotkin, Peter 64
Kuhn, Thomas viii, xi, 24

Lessig, Lawrence 3, 37, 43
libertarianism 23, 25, 64–67, 93
Lock, John 62

Madison, James 5, 8, 62–63
Magna Carta 32
Meade, James Edward 66–67, 94
media 6, 8, 16–17, 22, 28, 37, 99, 110
Mongolia 41
Mosca, Gaetano 14–15

Neolithic Revolution 9, 26
New England Townhalls 96

Owen, Robert 25, 64

Paris Accords 13–14
Paris Commune 22–23
Plato 15, 22, 57–61
Pluriverse xv
pollution xii, xiv, 106
Proudhon, Pierre-Joseph 64
public sphere 2, 29

Quebec 101

racism 8, 75–76, 78, 89, 91, 92, 100
Rawls, John xvii, 66–67, 78, 92, 95
recycling 100, 102–3, 111
Rome (ancient) 5, 28, 32, 60
Rousseau, Jean Jacques 4–5, 27

Scott, James 9, 15, 26
self-rule xv, 8–9, 26, 28, 31, 33, 65
Sen, Amartya xvii, 52, 67, 95
Senate 34, 37, 39
sexism 100
Smith, Adam 62–64, 94
Socrates 15, 22
Spanish Anarchism (1936) 24, 64
stakeholdership 18, 22, 33, 37–38, 42, 95, 110
statehood 87
state power 19, 25–26, 32
Switzerland 26, 32, 34, 39, 41, 51, 97

taxes xiii, xvi, 9, 13, 19, 48, 51–52, 54, 64, 104–5, 107
Thunberg, Greta 16
Tocqueville, Alexis de 32
Trump, Donald 1–3, 8, 12
Twin Oaks 27

Vermont 26, 30–31, 97

welfare vii, xiv, xvi, 19, 66, 102
Wintukua 26

Yachts xii, 105

Zapatistas 3, 26, 47

www.ingramcontent.com/pod-product-compliance
Lightning Source LLC
Chambersburg PA
CBHW030234170426
43201CB00006B/221